— Healthy Cooking —

GLUTEN FREE
COOKBOOK

ɔ.

‎e sh

T

Healthy Cooking

GLUTEN FREE
COOKBOOK

Paul Morgan

AN OCEANA BOOK

This edition published by Silverdale Books,
an imprint of Bookmart Ltd., in 2006

Bookmart Ltd.
Blaby Road
Wigston
Leicester
LE18 4SE

ISBN 1-84509-232-5

QUMHCGF

Manufactured in Singapore by
Pica Digital Pte. Ltd.
Printed in Singapore by
Star Standard Industries (Pte) Ltd

It is always sensible to consult your doctor before changing your diet
regime, but it is essential to do so if you suffer from any medical
condition or are taking medication of any kind. If you are concerned about
any symptoms that develop after changing your diet, consult your doctor
immediately. Information is given without any guarantees on the part of the
author and publisher, and they cannot be held responsible for the
contents of this book.

CONTENTS

INTRODUCTION

If you are reading this, it is likely that you have either been diagnosed with coeliac disease, the condition in which your body reacts against the dietary protein gluten, or are worried – probably because of your family medical history – that you will develop the condition. You would not be alone: between 1 in 250 to 300 Europeans and 1 in 133 Americans has coeliac disease, and about 10 per cent of the parents, brothers and sisters and children of those who are affected by the condition will also develop it.

There is only one treatment for coeliac disease, and it is to avoid gluten in your diet. It is not easy to do this and still eat satisfying, tasty meals; however, as this book will show, it is far from impossible to break the gluten-free taste-barrier. This is a healthy eating cookbook, though, and the omission of gluten from your diet makes it even more difficult to eat healthily. Again, the challenge can be overcome. But what is a healthy diet?

For 25 years or more, theories about what constitutes a healthy diet have chopped and changed.

A diet high in fresh vegetables and fruit, and low in salt, will help protect against many cancers.

Take your heart and circulatory system, for example. First, all fat was considered to be bad for you – then it was found that some types of fat can protect your heart. Then butter was considered bad, while margarine was thought to be good for you – but after a while, scientists discovered that margarine contained substances called trans fatty acids, which are extremely bad for you. At the same time, all cholesterol was once considered dangerous, but now we know that one type of cholesterol is, in fact, very good for you.

And for 17 of these 25 years, scientists tended to mock the insistent claims made by practitioners of fringe and alternative medicine to the effect that people could prevent cancer from developing if they ate the correct diet. But in 1997, the doubters were proved wrong, when the World Cancer Research Fund and the American Institute for Cancer Research (AIRC) published a joint study that was the culmination of 15 years of research. In it, they stated

'The panel found that . . . inappropriate diets cause around one-third of all cancer deaths . . . . [it] estimates that 30 to 40 per cent of cancer cases throughout the world are preventable by feasible dietary means'.

You could be forgiven for being confused. But now, after years of research, scientists have a fairly clear picture of the relationship between nutrition and disease. The basic facts are now known: it is beyond question that by eating a healthy diet and avoiding some foods while emphasising others you can significantly reduce your chances of developing diseases of the heart and arteries and contracting many types of cancer.

This book will show you how to do just that – while staying gluten-free. First we will look at what coeliac disease is and how it affects the body. Then we will show how the make-up of some foods can cause disease while the chemical basis of other foods can prevent it. Then you can choose from a range of mouth-watering, gluten-free, healthy recipes. It may be a cliché, but like many clichés it is true: when it comes to your health, you really are what you eat!

WHAT IS COELIAC DISEASE?

Coeliac disease, also known as gluten-sensitive enteropathy (GSE), coeliac sprue and non-tropical spruc, is caused by an autoimmune response – think of it as an allergy – to gluten, a protein found in wheat, rye and barley. The allergic response damages the tiny projections (villi) in the small intestine through which nutrients are absorbed. The result is that insufficient nutrients can be absorbed, and this causes serious malnutrition and a range of other symptoms, and can lead to some serious complications (see pages 7 and 8).

Nobody knows what causes coeliac disease, though it is known that it has a genetic component and runs in families: if you are a first degree relative (a parent, brother, sister or a child) of someone who has coeliac disease there is a 1 in 10 chance that you will develop it. What is also known is that it is more common in people who have another autoimmune disorder, such as rheumatoid arthritis, type 1 diabetes, lupus erythematosus and autoimmune thyroid disease.

The condition is diagnosed by means of a simple blood test, in which the blood is checked for the presence of specific protective chemicals (antibodies) that are produced as part of the body's response to gluten. If they are found, it may be necessary for doctors to take a small sample of intestinal tissue for examination. It is sensible to ask your doctor whether you should have the blood test if you think that you may be at risk of the disease because of your family medical history. This is because it is possible to have coeliac disease without having any digestive symptoms if sufficient of your small intestine is undamaged, yet still be at risk of complications.

The only treatment for coeliac disease is to adopt a gluten-free diet. Once a coeliac sufferer has done this (but only after consulting a doctor), the symptoms will begin to die down within a few weeks and your villi will start to heal, though this process takes several years in older people. Vitamin and mineral supplements may also be prescribed to correct any deficiencies that have built up. But the gluten-free diet is then for life – even small traces of gluten can damage your intestines.

WHAT ARE THE SYMPTOMS AND COMPLICATIONS?

Coeliac disease is unusual, in that its symptoms are extremely varied – in fact, there may be no symptoms at all, because damage to the intestines is only limited, but in this case there is still a risk of complications. Often, the disease mimics other conditions, such as irritable bowel syndrome, anaemia and skin disorders. Symptoms may develop at any time of life, and it is thought that breastfeeding babies for longer may delay their onset. They may include:

- general fatigue
- irritability or depression
- abdominal cramps, bloating and wind
- weight loss
- persistent diarrhoea
- pale, foul-smelling stools
- muscle cramps
- joint pain
- skin rashes
- seizures.

If you suffer from any of these symptoms, consult your doctor.

COMPLICATIONS

A number of complications can arise with coeliac disease, but they are usually resolved when a gluten-free diet is adopted. They include:

- osteoporosis – a loss of bone density that results from too little vitamin D and calcium being absorbed, making bones fragile; the bones may also become soft (osteomalacia)

- lactose intolerance – the sugar lactose, found in dairy products, may cause bloating, wind and diarrhoea; this usually clears up with a gluten-free diet, but does not always do so

- nerve damage – tingling in the extremities and an increased risk of developing epilepsy

- cancer – an increased risk of developing bowel cancer

- dermatitis herpetiformis – a chronic skin rash, with groups of watery blisters that itch; this is the result of a different type of immune response to gluten, but often coexists with coeliac disease.

WHAT IS A GLUTEN-FREE DIET?

It sounds simple enough. If wheat, rye and barley contain gluten, then they must be not be eaten. Instead, you should eat foods that do not contain gluten, such as meat, fish, cheese, eggs, milk, vegetables and fruit. Unfortunately, it is not as easy as it sounds.

The problem is that wheat – and so gluten – is used, in the form of wheat flour, in the production not only of cakes, biscuits, pastries, puddings, pasta, pies, sauces and gravies but also of manufactured and processed foods, as a binder, filler or carrier of flavourings. (Luckily, as you will discover later in this book, processed foods rarely play a part in a healthy diet.) And even if it is not used directly, the gluten in wheat can contaminate foods. Oats, for example, do not naturally contain gluten, but can become contaminated if they pass through the same milling machinery as wheat. (It is extremely hard to obtain uncontaminated oats, so coeliac sufferers are advised not to eat them.)

The question then arises: how can I tell what I can eat? Again, the answer is complicated. A product's label will reveal whether wheat, wheat starch or wheat flour is used, but small amounts, present in another ingredient, are often not listed. Instead, look out for products identified as 'gluten-free' – these are made with specially treated wheat starch and accord to the International Gluten-free Standard, known as the Codex Alimentarius, which certifies that the product contains less than 0.05g of nitrogen per 100 g. Most people with coeliac disease can eat these products, but some, known as "super-sensitives" cannot tolerate them and require a diet that is both gluten-free and completely wheat-free. Products that satisfy this requirement use gluten-free foods such as potato, rice, soya or maize instead of wheat starch. A range of basic foods is on the market, such as bread, flour and pasta, as well as some luxury ones – in the UK they are available on prescription.

Otherwise, it is best to rely on the advice of your dietician, or consult the specialist websites that contain lists of gluten-free and wheat-free foods: in the UK, www.coeliac.co.uk; in the US, www.csaceliacs.com; and in Australia, www.coeliac.org.au.

A HEALTHY DIET

A gluten-free diet does not guarantee good health – far from it. It is just as easy to develop heart problems and some cancers on a gluten-free diet as on a normal one. In the following pages, we are going to explore the link between nutrition and disease and show how you can improve your health by changing your diet. Essentially, it limits your intake of certain carbohydrates and fats, and maximizes your daily intake of life-preserving vegetables and fruits and gluten-free fibre (such as rice bran) and grains (such as corn, buckwheat, millet and rice).

DIET AND BLOOD PRESSURE

Most people know that high blood pressure puts the whole circulatory system at risk, causing a build-up of fatty plaques in the arteries and leading to heart disease or a stroke. What is less well known is that it is also a risk factor for certain cancers – in particular, for kidney cancer. But what is high blood pressure and what causes it?

Pressure points

The phrase 'high blood pressure' means that the force that blood exerts on the walls of arteries as it flows through them is higher than is normal. It is estimated that between 10 and 20 per cent of the population have high blood pressure, but many people do not know that they have it – there are often no symptoms, which is why it is sometimes known as 'the silent killer'.

Atherosclerosis is the condition in which plaques (atheromata) form on the inner walls of arteries. The plaques consist of dead cells, fibrous tissue and calcium, among other things, but primarily contain cholesterol. They can cause the arteries to harden, narrow and become less flexible (arteriosclerosis), or block them. If atherosclerosis blocks the coronary arteries, which supply the heart with blood, the result will be a heart attack. Sometimes, too, pieces of plaque can break off (thrombi) and be carried around the circulatory system to block other, smaller blood vessels – if these supply blood to the brain, the result could be a stroke.

The nature of the link between atherosclerosis and high blood pressure is complex. Each condition can cause the other one, but generally both develop as a result of lifestyle factors and the natural processes of ageing (some people also have an inherited predisposition to them). Smoking, drinking excessive amounts of alcohol, obesity, high stress levels and the presence of other conditions, such as diabetes, play a major part in the development of both problems, but so, too, does your diet.

Cakes, puddings and biscuits should be avoided and replaced with fruit, yoghurts and low fat desserts that do not contain gluten and too much sugar.

The culprits

The main dietary culprits when it comes to developing atherosclerosis and high blood pressure – and so some cancers - are saturated fats, trans fats, dietary cholesterol and salt. But some foods can actually prevent both problems. The trick is to know which foods to choose and which to avoid – and what follows will show you.

FATS AND CHOLESTEROL

For many years, scientists believed that the cholesterol that you eat is the villain of the piece when it comes to heart disease. In fact, about 75 per cent of the cholesterol in your blood is manufactured by your liver, while only 25 per cent of it is in your diet. And the liver uses dietary fat to make cholesterol. When this was appreciated, the emphasis moved to eating a low-fat and low-cholesterol diet. But then it was discovered that it is not only the amount of fat in your diet that is important, but how much of which type of fat you eat – and there are three main types of fat: saturated fats, unsaturated fats and trans fats.

Saturated fats are found in meat, poultry, lard and whole-milk dairy products, such as cheese, milk, butter and cream, but high levels are also found in some vegetable oils, such as coconut and palm oil.

Unsaturated fats, which typically are liquid at room temperature, are found in plant and vegetable oils, such as olive, peanut, sesame, safflower, corn, sunflower, canola and soybean oil, and in avocados, oily fish (in the form or omega 3 fatty acid) and nuts and seeds.

Trans fats are man-made – a by-product of heating vegetable oils in the presence of hydrogen (which is why they are often referred to as 'hydrogenated vegetable oils' on product labels). They are found in commercial baked goods – even gluten-free ones, such as biscuits, snack foods, processed foods and commercially prepared fried foods, such as crisps. Some margarines also contain high levels of trans fats, especially brands that are 'stick' margarines – spreadable ones have less high levels as they are less hydrogenated (hydrogenation makes the fat hard at room temperature).

Where cholesterol comes in

Your body needs cholesterol to function correctly – it is involved in the production of hormones, the body's chemical messengers, as well as bile and vitamin D, and is found in every part of the body. For this reason, it is manufactured in the liver – and the liver uses fats to make it. If you eat too much saturated fat, the liver produces too much cholesterol. Unfortunately, cholesterol is a soft, waxy substance that can stick to the lining of blood vessels and obstruct them if there are high levels of it in the blood.

As we have seen, liver-produced cholesterol, and so the cholesterol that is ultimately the result of fat consumption, accounts for around 75 per cent of the cholesterol found in your blood. The remaining 25 per cent comes from the cholesterol you eat. Dietary cholesterol is found in eggs, dairy products, meat, poultry, fish and shellfish, but the highest levels are found in egg yolks, meats such as liver and kidneys and shellfish. Vegetable, fruits, nuts, grains and cereals contain no cholesterol.

'Good' and 'bad' cholesterol

Cholesterol is carried around the body by chemicals called lipoproteins. There are two types: low-density lipoprotein (LDL) and high-density lipoprotein (HDL). If there is too much of the cholesterol carried by LDL, known as 'bad' cholesterol, plaque builds up on arterial walls. But HDL carries cholesterol away from the arteries to the liver, which breaks it down so that it

can be excreted from the body; for this reason, HDL cholesterol is said to be 'good' cholesterol. It has now been demonstrated that saturated fats, and, in particular, trans fats, increase the blood levels of harmful LDL cholesterol and lower levels of beneficial HDL cholesterol, while unsaturated fats have the opposite effect.

To conclude, then, a healthy diet, which helps prevent heart disease and some cancers, is one that has low levels of saturated and trans fats, and high levels of unsaturated fats.

FOODS TO CHOOSE
(Containing unsaturated fat)

Vegetable oils – pure olive, peanut, walnut, sesame, corn, soybean, sunflower and safflower oils

Avocados

Oily fish – salmon, mackerel, tuna, herrings and so on

Nuts

Spreadable, unsaturated margarine

FOODS TO USE SPARINGLY
(Containing saturated fat)

Whole-fat milk (skimmed milk is preferable)

Butter, cream, cheese, full-fat yoghurt (low-fat is preferable), ice cream

Meat – beef, lamb and pork

Poultry – battery-farmed chicken (free-range is preferable), goose, duck and turkey (wild game, such as rabbit, wild duck and venison, is better)

Lard

Eggs (especially ones from battery-farmed chickens)

Coconut oil and palm oil

FOODS TO AVOID (EVEN IF GLUTEN-FREE)
(Containing trans fats)

Ready-made commercial foods – cakes, biscuits and snack foods

Processed foods – sausages, pâté, scotch eggs, pies and so on

Commercially prepared fried foods – crisps, battered fish and chips

Hard margarine

DIET AND CANCER

Contrary to popular belief, carcinogens (cancer-causing chemicals) in the diet are only very rarely a cause of cancer. The 15-year analysis of statistics relating to food intake and diet undertaken by the AICR has demonstrated that in a hugely significant proportion of cancer cases, the changes are the result of eating an unhealthy diet. Unfortunately, nobody knows for certain why this should be – perhaps ongoing research will provide the answer.

Here is a summary of the main findings of the AICR's study linking a reduction in the risks of specific cancers to dietary measures:

- **Lung cancer:** the most common cause of lung cancer is tobacco smoking, but a diet rich in vegetables and fruits may prevent between 20 and 33 per cent of cases in both smokers and non-smokers

- **Stomach cancer:** diets high in vegetables and fruits, and low in salt, together with the routine use of freezing and refrigeration of perishable foods may prevent between 66 and 75 per cent of cases

- **Breast cancer:** a diet rich in vegetables and fruit, an appropriate body weight and an avoidance of alcohol may prevent between 10 and 20 per cent of cases (more if this diet is adopted early in life)

- **Bowel cancer:** a diet high in vegetables and gluten-free fibre and low in meat and alcohol may, together with regular physical exercise, prevent 66 to 75 per cent of cases

- **Mouth and throat cancer:** a diet high in vegetables and fruit, and low in alcohol consumption may – in the absence of tobacco smoking – prevent between 30 and 50 per cent of cases

- **Liver cancer:** avoidance of alcohol (and of aflatoxins, found in a mould that grows on some nuts) may prevent between 33 and 66 per cent of cases.

The message seems fairly clear: if you smoke, stop now; moderate your alcohol intake; cut down on the amount of meat you eat; and emphasize vegetables and fruit in your diet. It is particularly important that you take these steps if you have a family history of cancer, because genetic predisposition is a major risk factor for developing cancer.

Smoking is one of the most common causes of cancer. Stop now and replace this with a healthy diet rich in antioxidants from fruit and vegetables.

ANTIOXIDANTS, VITAMINS AND MINERALS

Many of our bodily structures can be damaged by the presence of what are known as 'free radicals' – technically speaking, these are atoms that have unpaired electrons. The most common free radical is radical oxygen, which can damage cells, causing them to develop cancerous changes, and increase the likelihood that cholesterol forms fatty plaques in arteries, leading to heart disease.

When this was realised, in the 1990s, nutritionists started to look at the antioxidants, which combat radical oxygen and so help prevent cancer and heart disease. The most important antioxidants amongst them are vitamins C and E, beta-carotene (a precursor to vitamin A) and lycopene. Soon antioxidant supplements became increasingly popular, and today some 30 per cent of Americans take them. Unfortunately, they do not reduce the risks of cancer, heart disease or stroke, as a series of studies, and meta-studies (that is, studies of studies) have shown.

Nevertheless, it has been shown that a diet that is high in antioxidants is protective against cancer and heart disease. The answer to this conundrum is thought to be that in practice the effect of dietary antioxidant relies on the interaction between the antioxidants and other dietary ingredients: minerals, perhaps, or fibre. So it is important to eat a diet rich in antioxidants – that means richly coloured fruit and vegetables that contain chemicals called flavonoids, such as apricots, blueberries, bilberries, broccoli, carrots, mangos, peppers and spinach, and, in particular, tomatoes (though these should be cooked to release maximum quantities of flavonoids).

Vitamins and minerals

Every one of our body's systems need vitamins and minerals to function. Vitamins act as catalysts, initiating and controlling chemical reactions in the body, while minerals also play a vital part in body chemistry. Only small amounts of them are needed – they are known as micronutrients – and they must be obtained from our diet, because the body cannot manufacture them. If you follow the rules for healthy eating given in this book, and take a multivitamin supplement every day, as a precaution, you should absorb all the vitamins and minerals that your body requires. But sometimes the way that we treat and

A bowl of fresh fruit is lovely and refreshing, full of vitamins and minerals.........and no fat or gluten.

Richly coloured vegetables contain high levels of antioxidants that help prevent against cancer, and look wonderfully appetizing in salads and dips.

cook food reduces its content of micronutrients. Follow these rules to make sure that you can meet your body's requirements.

- Avoid even gluten-free processed foods, and canned foods in particular, because these can be low in vitamin content.

- Always use fresh or frozen fruit and vegetables, because vitamin levels decrease as these foods age. It is not generally realised that freezing preserves vitamin content, but chilling fruit and vegetables in a refrigerator before heating them can reduce levels of vitamins such as vitamin C and folic acid by up to 30 per cent. Remember that frozen vegetables – peas, especially – are often more vitamin-rich than fresh ones, because they are frozen immediately after being picked.

- Keep all foods away from heat, light and air, all of which reduce levels of vitamin C and the B vitamins. Store vegetables in airtight bags.

- Use the skin of fruits and vegetables wherever possible. Instead of peeling, wash or scrub them – most of the nutritional value of fruits and vegetables is contained in the skin or the area underneath it.

- Keep the water you have used to cook vegetables and use it as a base for stock or sauces – otherwise you will lose the valuable vitamins and minerals that have dissolved into the water.

- Unless your dietician has advised otherwise, or prescribed special supplements, take a daily multivitamin supplement – it can be hard to obtain sufficient quantities of some vitamins, such as B12 and folic acid from your diet; and fibre-rich foods contain chemicals called phytates, which can bind with some minerals and interfere with their absorption. But think of it as a nutritional safety net, rather than as a substitute for healthy eating.

VITAMIN– AND MINERAL–RICH FOODS

(NB Pre-menopausal women and women taking HRT should eat more of foods containing vitamins that are depleted by the female hormone oestrogen.)

Vitamin A (antioxidant)
Retinol: butter, cod liver oil and cheese
Beta-carotene: apricots, cantaloupe, carrots, kale, peach, peas, spinach and sweet potatoes

Vitamin B1
Beans, brown rice, milk, oatmeal, vegetables, whole grains and yeast (depleted by alcohol, caffeine, exposure to air and water, food additives and oestrogen)

Vitamin B2
Eggs, fish, meat, milk, vegetables and whole grains (depleted by alcohol, caffeine, oestrogen and zinc)

Vitamin B3
Avocado, eggs, fish, meat, peanuts, prunes, seeds and whole grains (destroyed by canning and some sleeping pills; depleted by alcohol and oestrogen)

Vitamin B5
Bran, eggs, green vegetables, meat, whole grains and yeast (destroyed by canning)

Vitamin B6
Avocado, bananas, cabbage, cantaloupe, fish, milk, eggs, seeds and wheat bran (destroyed by alcohol, heat, oestrogen, and processing techniques during production of commercial food)

Vitamin B folic acid
Apricots, avocados, beans, carrots, green vegetables, melons, oranges and whole wheat (destroyed by commercial food processing techniques, cooking and exposure to water and air, depleted by alcohol)

Vitamin B12
Dairy products, fish and meat (depleted by alcohol, exposure to sunlight and water, oestrogen and sleeping tablets)

Vitamin C (antioxidant)
Broccoli, cabbage, cauliflower, citrus fruits, green peppers, spinach, tomatoes and potatoes (destroyed by boiling, exposure to air and carbon dioxide and long storage; depleted by alcohol, aspirin, oestrogen, stress and tobacco)

Vitamin D
Cod liver oil, dairy products and oily fish (depleted by lack of sunlight)

Vitamin E (antioxidant)
Almonds, broccoli, eggs, kale, oats, olive oil, peanuts, soybeans, seeds, spinach and wheat germ (destroyed by commercial food processing techniques, freezing, heat, oxygen and chlorine; depleted by smoking and use of contraceptive pills)

Vitamin K
Broccoli, cod liver oil, eggs, green vegetables, live yoghurt, tomatoes and whole grains

Magnesium
Bitter chocolate, brown rice, nuts, soybeans and whole wheat (depleted by caffeine and stress)

Zinc (antioxidant)
Eggs, meat, mushrooms, yeast and whole grains (inhibited by caffeine and smoking)

Potassium
Avocados, bananas, dried fruit, green vegetables, nuts and potatoes (lost in diarrhoea and sweat)

Selenium (antioxidant)
Broccoli, onions, tomatoes, tuna and wheat germ

TOO MUCH CAN BE DANGEROUS

Many people take high doses of vitamin supplements, without having taken medical advice. But doing so can be dangerous, because in many cases the effects of high doses are not known, and in some cases the effects have been confirmed to be dangerous. For example, it was once thought that very high doses of vitamin E might help prevent heart disease, but several studies have failed to show this and a recent study suggests that they may make heart failure more likely. And the list goes on: too much calcium can lead to lethargy, confusion and coma; excess vitamin B6 can cause a nerve disorder that leads to loss of feeling in the arms and legs; too much beta carotene can increase the risk of contracting lung cancer in smokers; high doses of vitamin A can increase the risk of cardiovascular disease and can damage your liver; excessive doses of vitamin C can cause abdominal pain, nausea and diarrhoea; and so on.

The message is clear: do not take high-dose vitamin supplements unless they have been prescribed by your doctor – you can obtain all the antioxidants, vitamins and minerals you need by eating a healthy diet and taking a daily multivitamin supplement.

CARBOHYDRATES

Carbohydrates are the body's primary source of fuel and are an essential part of a healthy diet. There are three types of carbohydrate: sugars, fibre and starch, and all of them are built from molecules of sugar. They used to be described as 'complex' or 'simple' carbohydrates, depending on whether they were simple forms of sugar or consisted of linked forms of sugar, and it was believed that simple carbohydrates should be avoided and complex ones preferred.

Today this categorization is now longer used. Instead, nutritionists classify carbohydrates according to their glycaemic index, or 'GI'. During the digestive process, carbohydrates are broken down into the simplest forms of sugar, and the glycaemic index measures how quickly this happens and so how fast levels of sugar in the blood rise – a high GI value means that the carbohydrate raises these levels very quickly.

The significance of this is that the pancreas starts to produce the hormone insulin in response to rising blood sugar levels, and this promotes the uptake of sugar by the body's cells and reduces sugar levels in the blood. If you continually eat foods with a high GI – and if you have a hereditary disposition to the problem or are overweight and inactive – the levels of both insulin and sugar in your blood remain high, and you develop what is known as insulin resistance (the body loses its sensitivity to insulin, so more and more is needed). This can not only lead to type 2 diabetes, but result in high blood pressure, low levels of 'good' cholesterol (see page 10) and the risk of heart disease.

There is some evidence that eating high GI carbohydrates may also be linked to an increased risk of colorectal, breast and pancreatic cancer, though the link has not been conclusively proved as yet. Until more is known, though, it would be sensible to choose a diet that emphasises low and medium GI foods.

High or low?

In essence, whether a food has a high or low GI depends on how quickly its carbohydrates are converted to simple sugar during the digestive process. Foods that have not been processed still contain their original fibre, which slows down the rate at which carbohydrates are converted to simple sugars and so also slows down the rate at which sugar enters the bloodstream; conversely, the carbohydrates in processed foods have already been partly broken down, meaning that their sugar enters the bloodstream relatively quickly.

However, the type of starch in the food is important, too: potatoes, for example, contain a starch that is broken down quickly during digestion. Other factors affecting the GI value are: ripeness – ripe fruit has a higher GI than unripe fruit; acidity – vinegar and lemon juice delay stomach emptying and so reduce the GI value; and the size of food particles – small particles are more easily absorbed and increase the GI value.

Low GI foods include soy, chickpeas, fruit, milk and rice bran; medium ones include corn, nuts, and orange juice; while high GI foods include potatoes, rice and gluten-free bread. It might seem a daunting prospect to exist solely on low GI foods, but it is not necessary to do so. This is because eating a low GI food reduces the GI value of high GI foods when they are eaten at the same time – if, for example, you eat a gluten-free biscuit (high GI) with a glass of milk (low GI) your blood sugar levels will not go up as quickly – what is known as the overall 'glycaemic load' (GL) is reduced. In essence, the equation reads 'high GI + low GI = medium GI' – so if you plan your menus carefully you can still eat some high GI foods.

PLUSES AND A MINUS

Maximizing the amount of low GI foods in your diet and minimizing the amount of high GI ones has numerous benefits:

- the slow breakdown of low GI foods during digestion and the gradual release of their sugars into your bloodstream means that you will not feel the 'sugar let-down' that comes when quick-release sugars are used up; in turn this means that you will not need to have another 'sugar hit' as quickly, so you will eat less – which means that you will lose weight (about 450 to 900 g a week)
- the slow release of sugars into your bloodstream increases your physical endurance
- a low GI diet increases the body's sensitivity to insulin (see page 15), which reduces the risk of developing insulin resistance, and so diabetes and heart disease
- including a larger proportion of low GI foods means that you will reduce your intake of 'bad' saturated fats and trans fats (see page 9) and lessen the likelihood that you will develop heart disease
- there is some evidence that a low GI diet may help prevent some cancers
- so long as you choose low GI foods, you can snack between meals
- a low GI diet leads to increased levels of serotonin in the brain – and serotonin makes you feel good
- a low GI diet can easily be followed for life, unlike other fad diets.

But, in case low GI diet seems too good to be true, there is just one minus:

- healthy though they may be, even low-GI foods contain calories, so if you eat too many of them you will not lose weight: you still have to control portion sizes.

FOODS TO CHOOSE
(Low glycaemic index carbohydrates)
Rice bran
Buckwheat
Legumes – chickpeas, lentils
Some fruits – apples, citrus, berries, peaches, pears, plums and rhubarb
Some vegetables – avocados, aubergines, beans (runner and green), broccoli, cabbage, cauliflower, carrots, celery, courgettes, cucumber, leeks, onions, lettuce, mushrooms, olives, peas, peppers, spinach and tomatoes

FOODS TO USE SPARINGLY
(Medium glycaemic index carbohydrates)
Nuts
Basmati or long-grained rice and wild rice
Corn – cornmeal, corn oil and sweetcorn
Some fruits – apricots, bananas, melon, dried fruit, pineapples and mangos
Some vegetables – new potatoes, sweet potatoes, beetroot and artichokes
Honey

FOODS TO AVOID
(High glycaemic index carbohydrates
Gluten-free breakfast cereals – sugar-coated corn or rice cereals
Gluten-free white bread, cakes, cookies, bagels, buns, muffins, pancakes and doughnuts
Some fruits – dates, prunes and watermelon
Some vegetables – broad beans, potatoes (when mashed, baked, fried, or roasted), parsnips and swede
Sugar – table, glucose, treacle and molasses
Gluten-free tomato ketchup

SALT
The more salt you eat, the more your body retains fluid, and the more fluid there is, the harder your heart has to work to pump blood around your body. And the result of this increase in the heart's work rate is high blood pressure and the risk, over time, of developing heart failure. High levels of salt in your diet are also linked to the incidence of certain cancers – in particular to stomach cancer.

THE DANGERS OF BEING OVERWEIGHT

Being overweight – always a possibility, even on a gluten-free diet – brings with it the dangers of many health problems, including an increased risk of developing colonic and rectal cancer, but if you carry the extra pounds on your waist – in the classic 'beer belly' – you are far more at risk of heart disease or diabetes. In fact, men with waists of more than 101 cm (40 inches) and women with waists of more than 89 cm (35 inches) are at between double and quadruple the risk of developing them.

The reason is that fat that is stored around the stomach secretes hormones that play havoc with the production of insulin, the pancreatic hormone that controls blood sugar levels. As a result 'insulin resistance' develops, leading to diabetes, high blood pressure and high cholesterol levels. The healthiest and most-effective way to lose weight is to follow the low GI diet.

CHECK THE LABEL

Food manufacturers are starting to note GI values on product labels, and the practice is likely to become more and more widespread. (In fact, the World Health Authority advises that GI values should be stated and that the values for 'complex carbohydrates' and sugars, which are used currently, are dropped.) But how do you interpret the figures?

The answer is that the maximum GI value, which is based on pure glucose, is 100, and that foods are said to have a low GI when the value is 55 or less; to be medium GI when the value is between 56 and 69; and high GI when the value is 70 or more. Remember that, ideally, you should stick to low GI foods; failing that, you should combine medium and low GI foods; and that if you ever eat high GI foods you should combine them with low GI ones.

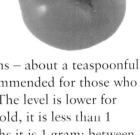

Doctors recommend that our daily intake of salt should be less than 6 grams – about a teaspoonful. Even less salt than this is recommended for those who already have heart problems. The level is lower for children, too: up to 6 months old, it is less than 1 gram; between 7 and 12 months it is 1 gram; between 1 and 3 years it is 2 grams; between 4 and 6 it is 3 grams; and between 7 and 10 years it is 5 grams. Worryingly, one small can of gluten-free baked beans served on a piece of toast made from gluten-free, white, supermarket bread can contain around 0.9 grams – half of a toddler's recommended daily intake.

Hidden salt

The 6 gram target sounds an easy enough one to achieve, but in fact it is very tall order. The reason is that this target refers to our total salt intake, not just to the salt that we add to our food, and there is a considerable amount of salt hidden in the foods many of us eat. Processed foods are mainly to blame – in fact, researchers estimate that around 75 per cent of our salt intake comes from them.

It is obvious that some foods contain high salt levels: salted nuts, olives and anchovies, for example, all taste, and are, salty. But bacon, cheese and smoked meat and fish contain salt, too. And some brands of gluten-free foods, such as biscuits and breakfast cereals, are also surprisingly high in salt.

The only way to check which processed foods are high in salt is to read product labels carefully. It is easy to come unstuck when you do this, however, because some labels do not refer to the product's salt content but to its sodium content (salt is made up of sodium and chloride). The two values are not the same – in fact, you have to multiply the sodium value by 2.5 to obtain the real salt content.

Reducing your salt intake

If you cut down on salt, your blood pressure will fall within weeks, even if it was not too high in the first place. And that means that your risk of developing heart disease, having a stroke or developing certain cancers will also fall.

Many people think that their food will lack taste if they cut down on salt, but this is a myth. You may find that your diet is a little bland for the first week or so, but your taste buds soon adapt. Adopt these salt reduction strategies and you will find the process much more easy.

SALT SUBSTITUTES

Some people find that their food tastes a little bland when they switch to a low-salt diet, and even though their taste buds will adapt within a few weeks some people find that they need a little help to make the change. A number of salt substitutes are on the market, but these contain part sodium and part potassium and in certain circumstances it is possible to overload your body with potassium – consult your doctor before using a commercial salt substitute.

Make your own

This recipe for a salt substitute relies on the principle that a sour flavour is a good substitute for a salty one. It uses the grapefruit peel (or lemon or orange peel, for a weaker taste and citric acid crystal. Also known as 'sour salt' and 'lemon salt', these can be found in the baking section of supermarkets or in delicatessens.

Ingredients

- the peel of 1 grapefruit
- 1 tbsp ground allspice
- ½ tbsp citric acid crystals

Makes 3 tablespoons

Method

1 Peel the grapefruit as thinly as possible, then scrape away all the white parts. Dry the peel overnight near a source of heat.

2 Grind the dried peel in a coffee grinder or spice grinder, then combine it with the other ingredients. Put the mixture into a well-sealed bottle and shake well to mix. Store in a dry place.

Variations

Add a tablespoon of freshly ground black pepper to the mixture to make it into citrus pepper, an ideal seasoning for meat.

CALCULATE YOUR SALT INTAKE

If you must eat processed foods – and it can be hard not to – try to make sure that you stay within the recommended daily intake of 6 grams of salt. Read a product's label to find the number of grams of salt in 100 grams of the contents. If the quantity of sodium is given, multiply by 2.5 to calculate the actual salt content. (If the value is given in milligrams, or 'mg' divide by 1,000 to convert it to grams.)

Then look for the total weight of the contents, or estimate the proportion of them that you intend to use. Divide the weight that you will use by 100, then multiply by the number of grams of salt in each 100 grams and you will discover how much salt you will eat. The results can be surprising: one small (200g) tin of gluten-free baked beans can contain as much as 1.7 grams of salt – just under a third of your total recommended intake; one slice of white, refined, gluten-free bread contains 0.61 grams of salt – so just the bread making up a lunchtime sandwich could well account for just under a fifth of your total recommended intake.

- **Avoid** processed foods
- **Check** the salt levels of all commercially prepared foods, including everyday products such as bread
- **Throw** away your salt shaker
- **Make** your own salt-free stocks and sauces
- **Use** alternative seasonings, such as lemon juice, herbs and vinegar
- **Eat** fresh fruit (bananas and avocados in particular) and vegetables: the potassium they contain helps counter the effect of dietary salt
- **Do** not switch to sea salt, rock salt or garlic salt – they are not different to normal salt
- **Ask** your doctor whether salt substitutes are suitable for you.

FOODS TO AVOID
All types of salt – table, rock, sea and garlic
Obviously salty foods – anchovies and salted nuts

FOODS TO USE SPARINGLY
Commercially prepared gluten-free foods

PROTEIN

Protein, made up from chemicals called amino acids, make up the building blocks of all our body's tissues except stored fat. You need to eat a certain amount of protein every day – a minimum of one gram for every kilogram of body weight – to prevent the body from starting to break down tissue. And you need more than that if you want to build up healthy muscles and robust bones.

It is easy to get enough protein in your diet in Western industrialised societies, though hard to do so in developing countries. But the quantity of protein you eat is not the whole story. What is important is that you eat a variety of amino acids, which means protein from a variety of sources. This does not mean that it is essential to eat steaks, for example, because you can obtain a full range of proteins from vegetable and fruit sources, if you are a vegetarian. Variety is the watchword.

FOODS TO CHOOSE

('Good' protein – lower in saturated fats)
Vegetables – beans, brown rice, lentils, millet and pulses
Soybeans
Nuts – brazil, peanuts and pine-nuts
Seeds – sesame
Free-range chicken and turkey (but remove the skin)
Locally sourced lean cuts of non-intensively reared
Meats – beef, lamb, pork and veal
Free-range chicken eggs (but not duck or goose eggs)

FIBRE

Our bodies cannot digest some of the food that we eat, and it is this indigestible material that is known as dietary fibre. Most people know that a diet high in fibre is good for your bowel function and can protect against disorders of the intestines, such as cancer of the colon, but it is less well known that fibre can also lower the levels of cholesterol in your blood – which will lower your blood pressure and reduce you risk of developing other cancers, too.

There are two types of fibre: insoluble and soluble (the latter is so-called because it forms a gel when mixed with liquid). Insoluble fibre plays the main part in promoting bowel function, and high levels of it are found in foods such as rice, cabbage, carrots and so on. But it is soluble fibre that reduces blood cholesterol – though it is not clear how it does this. Gluten-free sources include lentils, beans, peas and fruits, and, conveniently, foods containing soluble fibre have a low GI rating.

FIVE A DAY

So it makes sense to increase your intake of foods rich in fibre, and especially of those rich in soluble fibre – generally, it is recommended that you should eat five portions of fibre-rich fruit and vegetables a day. And, of course, foods such as these are low in saturated fats and cholesterol. Make sure that you read labels carefully, though, because some commercial products that claim to be rich in fibre in fact contain very little of it.

FOODS TO CHOOSE

(High in soluble fibre)
Lentils, beans and peas
Apples, bananas, blueberries, oranges, pears and strawberries
Sweetcorn, spinach, spring greens and broccoli
Nuts – almonds, brazil, hazel, peanuts, pecan, pistachio and walnuts
Seeds – sesame, sunflower and pumpkin

FOODS TO USE

(High in insoluble fibre)
Gluten-free breads
Rice bran, brown rice
Fruit – both fresh and dried
All vegetables – but especially brussel sprouts, carrots, cabbage, okra, parsnips, sweetcorn, courgette, cucumber, celery, tomatoes and unpeeled potatoes

---

Avocados are rich in potassium, which helps counteract the effect of too much salt in your diet.

STRIKING A BALANCE

It is easy to decide which foods you should eat, but more difficult to decide how often to eat them. It is also hard to strike a nutritional balance between foods so that you obtain all the nutrients that your body demands in the correct quantities, yet protect your heart and arteries at the same time. And you will have noticed already from the tables in this book that certain foods are 'good' in the sense that they contain substantial quantities of a desirable ingredient, but 'not so good' in that they contain less desirable ingredients. So how do you do it?

The healthy eating pyramid shown on the opposite page indicates how often you should eat the different food groups. For instance, while certain foods are important as part of a balanced diet, they need to be eaten in moderation because of the health dangers associated with overindulgence.

Eating a balanced, nutritious diet that is free from gluten is a challenging task, but the recipes in this book show that it is achievable. Indeed, as will be demonstrated in the pages that follow, there is no reason why a diet free from gluten needn't be healthy, nutritious and full of flavour.

EXPLAINING THE SYMBOLS

SOLUBLE FIBRE

 HIGH

 MEDIUM

 LOW

UNSATURATED FAT

 HIGH

 MEDIUM

 LOW

PROTEIN

 HIGH

 MEDIUM

 LOW

CHOLESTEROL

 HIGH

 MEDIUM

 LOW

ANTIOXIDANT

 HIGH

 MEDIUM

 LOW

GLYCAEMIC INDEX

 HIGH

 MEDIUM

 LOW

SATURATED FAT

 HIGH

 MEDIUM

 LOW

INSOLUBLE FIBRE

 HIGH

 MEDIUM

 LOW

HEALTHY EATING PYRAMID

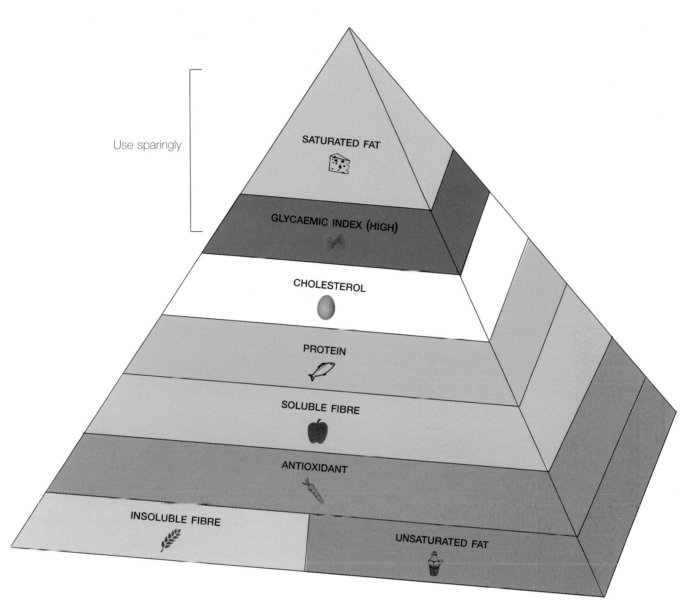

Use sparingly

SATURATED FAT

GLYCAEMIC INDEX (HIGH)

CHOLESTEROL

PROTEIN

SOLUBLE FIBRE

ANTIOXIDANT

INSOLUBLE FIBRE

UNSATURATED FAT

 Saturated Fat: Red meat, goose, duck, cheese, butter, cream, full-fat yoghurt

Soluble Fibre: Oats, barley, peas, beans, fruits (e.g. apples, oranges, bananas) nuts (2–3 times daily)

 Glycaemic Index (HIGH): Rice, white bread, potatoes, desserts, broad beans, prunes, watermelon and pasta

 Antioxidant: Spinach, broccoli, garlic, onions, red and orange vegetables and fruit, berries (at most meals)

 Cholesterol: Eggs, butter, cream, cheese, shellfish, pork, lamb, beef (0–1 times daily)

 Insoluble Fibre: Wheat bran, whole-wheat flour, wild rice, grains, cabbage, cauliflower, fruit skins (at most meals)

 Protein: Fish, shellfish, free-range chicken, rabbit, wild game, low-fat dairy (1–2 times daily)

 Unsaturated Fat: Olive oil, soya beans, avocado, peanuts, salmon, mackerel, tuna, sardines (1–2 times daily)

HOW TO COOK HEALTHILY

There is little point in choosing healthy ingredients and recipes if you cook them in a way that is in itself unhealthy. It is important to choose cooking methods that not only help reduce cholesterol and saturated fats and keep the calorie count low, but maximize the nutritional value of each dish. These techniques are effective, but may require a little practise:

- **Baking** – good for vegetables, fruit, poultry, and lean meat, as well as for puddings; you may need a little extra liquid
- **Braising or stewing** – brown first, on top of the stove, then cook in a small quantity of liquid; if you leave the dish in a refrigerator you can remove the chilled fat and then reheat it
- **Grilling** – on a rack, so that fat can drain away, and not in a direct flame
- **Microwaving** – place the food between two paper towels to drain fat away while it cooks
- **Poaching** – in a covered pan of the correct size, so that you use the minimum liquid
- **Roasting** – on a rack so that the food does not sit in fat; baste with fat-free liquids, such as wine or lemon juice
- **Sautéing** – use a high heat and a small amount of non-stick cooking spray, or just cook without spray if you have a good-quality non-stick pan
- **Steaming** – in a perforated basket over simmering water; add seasoning to the water for extra flavour
- **Stir-frying** – in a wok, using a small amount of non-stick cooking spray or a tiny amount of olive oil.

You can also increase flavour, reduce fat and salt content and make the most of your ingredients' nutritional value if you

Remember to:

- **Avoid** cooking methods that char food, such as barbecuing or grilling over a direct flame – charring produces carcinogens
- **Check** labels for common ingredients, such as soy sauce, baking soda and monosodium glutamate – these all contain high levels of sodium and should be used very sparingly, if at all
- **Make** your own stock rather than using pre-prepared cubes, which can be high in salt and may contain gluten
- **Steam** vegetables, for preference, in order to maximize both their flavour and nutritional value
- **Cook** lightly to preserve vitamin content (but cook meats and other foods that may harbour disease-producing organisms thoroughly)
- **Choose** extra virgin olive oil and vinegar rather than salted, pre-prepared salad dressings
- **Wash** canned vegetables before use – by doing so you can substantially reduce their salt content
- **Use** only one egg yolk when making scrambled eggs or omelettes, but mix in two or three extra egg whites
- **Trim** as much fat as you can from meat before you cook it and remove the skin from poultry
- **Choose** lean, low-fat meats, such as game (but, again, remember to remove the skin) and venison
- **Drain** oil from canned fish and rinse the fish in water before you use it
- **Use** herbs, wine and freshly ground pepper to enhance flavours; remember that a dash of vinegar or lemon juice will not only enhance flavour but reduce the GI rating of other ingredients.

Stocks can be made from almost anything. The shape of a stockpot permits the slow reduction of liquid, so it is as good for a long simmered meat stock as a quickly made seafood stock.

When making a vegetable stock make sure that the ones you use are fresh, as they will give a much better flavour.

MAKE YOUR OWN STOCK

Many stock cubes contain high levels of salt and low levels of nutrients. But nothing could be more simple than making your own stock, and if you make it in large batches you can freeze it for later use. You can use your stock as the basis for a delicious soup – serve it with a gluten-free roll – or as the basis of a nourishing stew or a piquant sauce.

VEGETABLE STOCK

Ingredients

3 large carrots, scrubbed but not peeled, coarsely chopped
1 turnip, coarsely chopped
2 onions, coarsely chopped
2 leeks, coarsely chopped
4 ribs of celery, including tops, coarsely chopped
coarsely chopped trimmings from cauliflower, spinach, broccoli or any other vegetables, so long as they are fresh and clean. Always use fresh vegetables.
125 g any dried beans, having been soaked overnight, if necessary; or use rice or barley
2 tbsp olive oil
1 bouquet garni, which includes 3 sprigs parsley, 1 sprig thyme and 1 bay leaf
1 tbsp peppercorns
Approx 3.6 litres of cold water for 900 g vegetables

Method

Warm the olive oil in a stockpot, add the vegetables and simmer, stirring continuously for 15 minutes until they start to colour slightly. Then add the water and the other ingredients and bring to simmering point. Simmer for at least 2 hours, adding more water if necessary. Then strain through cheesecloth or use a non-metallic colander. Use or freeze, as required.

Use the stocks for the basis of soups and stews. Soups are one of the easiest things to make, and can be made from nearly anything.

ingredients and more cold water to cover, if necessary. Return to simmering point and simmer for another 2 hours. Then strain through muslin or use a non-metallic colander. Refrigerate, and when stock has set remove any fat from the top. Use or freeze, as required.

FISH STOCK

Ingredients

900 g fish bones, heads (with gills removed) and tails (sole or plaice are tastiest, but any other white, non-oily fish will do)
1 large onion, coarsely chopped
2 shallots, coarsely chopped
2 ribs of celery, tops included, coarsely chopped
2 large carrots, scrubbed but not peeled, coarsely chopped
2 bay leaves
2 cloves
6 sprigs of parsley, coarsely chopped
1 tbsp peppercorns
Lemon rind from half a lemon
Cold water to cover

Method

Place everything in a stockpot and bring to simmering point – do not allow to boil. Simmer for 20–30 minutes, but no longer or the stock will become bitter. Strain through muslin or use a non-metallic colander. Reduce the strained stock by boiling, if required. Use or freeze as required.

CHICKEN STOCK

Ingredients

The bones of a chicken, and, if available, a ham bone or a veal knuckle (ask your butcher for one)
2 leeks, coarsely chopped
2 large carrots, scrubbed but not peeled, coarsely chopped
3 large onions, coarsely chopped
2 ribs of celery, tops included, coarsely chopped
6 sprigs of parsley, coarsely chopped
1 large clove of garlic
2 cloves
1 tbsp peppercorns
Lemon rind from half a lemon

Method

Place the bones in a stockpot and cover with cold water. Bring to simmering point – do not allow to boil. Simmer for at least an hour, then add all other

A HEALTHY LIFESTYLE

Eating a healthy diet is only one part of a healthy lifestyle. To reduce the risk of developing cancer and high blood pressure, to lower cholesterol levels, promote cardiovascular health and improve the quality of your life, you should also:

● **Give up smoking** – if you smoke, you are massively increasing the risk that you will develop lung, mouth, or throat cancer; and you are more than doubling the risk of having a heart attack, while making it less likely that you will survive a heart attack

● **Manage stress** – use relaxation techniques and anger-management methods to cope with stress and keep your blood pressure low

● **Lose weight** – if you are overweight, you are more at risk of developing certain cancers and between two and six times more likely to develop high blood pressure

● **Cut down on alcohol** – there's evidence to suggest that two units of alcohol, and especially of red wine, can reduce blood pressure, but more than this can increase the risk of certain cancers and actually raise blood pressure

● **Lead an active life** – even small amounts of physical activity, for example walking or gardening, can increase the number of calories that you burn and so help lose weight, as well as reducing the risk of developing cancers and heart disease.

Eating nutritiously is important, as well as getting plenty of exercise. Stick to low-fat foods and plenty of fruit and vegetables for a healthy and beneficial lifestyle.

TABLES

These tables give the nutritional values for the main ingredients used in the recipes that follow. To eat healthily and minimize your risk of developing cancer, the major part of your diet should consist of foods with a high fibre content, a low fat content, moderate protein levels, a low or medium glycaemic index and with plenty of antioxidants. Use the Healthy Eating Pyramid on p21 as a guide to proportions.

Remember that carrying excess weight is a major risk for developing ill health, and watch your calorie intake, too. Doctors recommend that men with a sedentary lifestyle – that of an office worker, say – should eat 2,700 calories a day, while women should eat 2,000. In order to lose weight gradually, at the rate of a pound a week, you need to reduce this figure by 500 calories.

Food	Quantity	Glycaemic index	Fat	Protein	Fibre	Calories
Meat and Dairy						
Cheese, feta	20 g	M	6	4	0	80
Cheese, reduced fat	20 g	M	4.5	7	0	70
Chicken skinless	100 g	L	5	30	0	150
Crème fraiche, low fat	100 g	M	17.5	3	0	800
Egg	1 medium	M	5.5	6	0	80
lean beef, lamb, pork	100 g	M	7	30	0	190
Milk, low fat	250 ml	L	2.5	8	0	102
Rabbit	100 g	L	4.5	30	0	160
Wild fowl	100 g	L	6	30	0	155
Yoghurt	100 g	L	0	5	0	40
Fish						
Herring, salmon	100 g	L	11	20	0	180
Mackerel	100 g	L	18	25	0	220
Sardine	100 g	L	2	15	0	65
Shellfish	100 g	L	1	15	0	105
Trout	100 g	L	6	20	0	155
Tuna	100 g	L	3	20	0	120
White fish	100 g	L	2	20	0	90

Prawns are an excellent low-calorie choice, and they are a rich source of protein, vitamins and minerals.

Food	Quantity	Glycaemic index	Fat	Protein	Fibre	Calories
Fruit						
Apple	1 medium	L	0	0.5	2	45
Apricot	3	M	0	1.5	2	30
Banana	1 small	M	0.5	1	1	90
Berries, fresh	100 g	L	0	0.5	1	30
Dried fruit	50 g	M	0	0.5	4	80
Grapefruit	half	L	0	0.5	1	30
Melon	slice	M	0	0.5	1	50
Nectarine, peach	1 medium	L	0	0.5	1	35
Orange	1 medium	L	0	1.5	3	50

Fruit is easily digested and has many health benefits.

Vegetables						
Avocado	½ medium	L	15	2	3.5	150
Aubergine	100 g	L	0	0.5	2	75
Beans	100 g	L	0.5	6	4	100
Beetroot	small	L	0	0.5	0.5	25
Broccoli	100 g	L	0	1.5	2.5	25
Cabbage	50 g	L	0	1	1	7
Carrot	50 g	L	0	0.5	1	12

Carrots are high in beta-carotene (providing vitamin A value) and cooking carrots actually enhances the digestibility of the beta-carotene.

Food	Quantity	Glycaemic index	Fat	Protein	Fibre	Calories
Vegetables (*continued*)						
Cauliflower	100 g	L	0	1	1.5	20
Green beans	100 g	L	0	1.5	2.5	20
Onions	medium	L	0	1	1.4	30
Peas	100 g	L	0	3.5	6	60
Peppers	100 g	L	0	1	2.5	30
Potatoes, new	3	M	0	1.5	3	100
Soyabean	100 g	L	7	8	6	120
Spinach	50 g cooked	L	0	1	1	10
Squash, butternut	100 g	M	0	1	1.5	30
Sweetcorn	100 g	M	0.5	2.5	1.5	95
Tofu	100 g	L	4	8	0	70
Tomato	medium	L	0	1	1	15

Eating raw onions can help to increase your high-density lipoprotein cholesterol (HDL) levels. This good type of cholesterol can help to keep blood pressure low, so reducing the risk of cardiovascular disease and stroke.

Peppers are low in calories and are especially rich in vitamins A and C. Surprisingly, a pepper contains three to four times more vitamin C than an orange. They do not contain any fat.

Food	Quantity	Glycaemic index	Fat	Protein	Fibre	Calories
Cereal, Nuts, Pulses						
Barley	50 g raw	L	1	2	1	140
Buckwheat	100 g	L	2.5	3	2.1	330
Chickpeas	100 g	L	3	5	4	110
Cornstarch	100 g	M	0.7	2	0.1	350
Lentils	100 g	L	0.5	8	2	100
Oats	50 g raw	L	1	4	3	140
Pasta, wholegrain	100 g	L	1	5	4	120
Rice, brown, basmati	100 g	M	0	3.5	1	200
Walnuts	2 tbsp	L	8	2	1	80
Wild rice	100 g	M	0	3	1	100

BREAKFASTS

HAM 'N' EGG COCOTTES

SERVES **4**

These light savouries are perfect for a special breakfast. Grated Gruyére cheese can be used in place of the Brie.

25 g ham, finely sliced

1 tbsp olive oil

225 g button mushrooms, wiped and sliced

freshly ground black pepper

4 medium eggs

4 tbsp crème fraîche

190 g Brie cheese, cubed

1 Preheat the oven to 190°C/gas mark 5 for 10 minutes before baking. Cut the ham into strips and use it to line four ramekin dishes. Warm the oil in a small frying pan and gently sauté the mushrooms for 2 minutes, drain on paper towels and place in the ramekin dishes. Season with the black pepper.

2 Break an egg into each dish, then pour over 1 tablespoon of the crème fraîche. Dot with the cubed cheese. Place on a roasting tray half filled with boiling water, then bake in the preheated oven for about 15–20 minutes or until set to personal preference. Serve with warm crusty gluten-free bread.

Variations

Use 3 skinned, seeded and chopped tomatoes in place of the mushrooms and sauté them gently for 1 minute. Or use 1 small onion, peeled and chopped, and sauté for 4–5 minutes or until softened.

NUTRITIONAL VALUES

HERB OMELETTE

SERVES **1**

To lift an omelette pan of any impurities simply line the pan with salt and set at a high heat for ten minutes. Tip away all the salt and lightly wipe with oil ready for your omelette mixture.

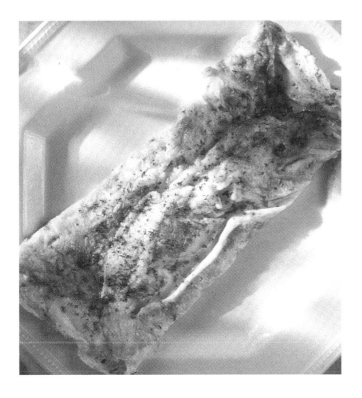

2 tbsp olive oil

2 eggs

1 tbsp chopped fresh parsley, chives, tarragon and chervil

Salt substitute (see page 18) and freshly ground black pepper to taste

1   Gently heat the oil.

2   Lightly beat the eggs – just enough to mix whites and yolks. Stir in a teaspoon of cold water.

3   Pour the egg mixture into the hot oil. Tilt the pan this way and that so the mixture spreads evenly.

4   Loosen the edges as they begin to set, then lower the heat and sprinkle the herbs on the egg. It should still be moist.

5   Fold one edge of the omelette into the middle. Fold the other over and slide it out of its pan. Sprinkle with the salt substitute and pepper and serve.

NUTRITIONAL VALUES

GRAPEFRUIT COCKTAILS

SERVES **4**

As for other citrus fruit, grapefruit is believed to slow down the rate of sugar metabolism. Here the fruit is transformed into three lively cocktails to start the day or begin a meal.

2 large juicy grapefruit

Peel the grapefruit and remove all the pith. Hold the fruit over a bowl and use a sharp serrated knife to cut in towards the middle of the fruit, removing the fleshy segments and leaving behind the membranes that separate them. Catch all the juice. This is the foundation for the three cocktails below.

GRAPE COCKTAIL

125 g seedless green grapes

2 kiwi fruit, peeled, halved and sliced

4 mint sprigs

Leave small grapes whole or halve larger ones and mix them with the grapefruit. Add the kiwi fruit and mint, then mix lightly.

MELON COCKTAIL

5 cm piece fresh ginger root, peeled and chopped

a little water

1 tbsp artificial sweetener

1 tbsp rose-water

¹/₄ honeydew melon

large wedge watermelon

1 Place the ginger in a small saucepan with water to cover. Bring to a boil, cover, and simmer for 30 minutes, making sure the water does not evaporate. At the end of cooking boil the ginger, if necessary, until the liquid is reduced to 2 tbsp or slightly less. Leave to cool, then stir n the artificial sweetener and rose-water.

2 Discard the seeds and peel from both types of melon, then cut them into small, neat cubes. Mix the melon with the grapefruit and strain the ginger juice over. Chill for at least 30 minutes before serving.

BANANA AND ORANGE COCKTAIL

2 oranges

2 bananas

2 tbsp slivered almonds, toasted

Remove the orange segments as for the grapefruit, then mix both citrus segments. (These may be covered and chilled ahead of time or overnight.) Just before serving, slice the bananas and mix them into the fruit. Spoon into dishes and top with almonds, then serve at once.

NUTRITIONAL VALUES

STRAWBERRIES WITH MELON AND ORANGE

This light refreshing breakfast salad is the perfect start to hot summer days.

450 g halved strawberries

1 small melon, balled

2 oranges

60 ml orange juice (optional)

mint leaves

1 Place the halved strawberries in a bowl with the melon balls. Peel the oranges, remove the pits and break into segments, then cut them in half or chop them roughly, depending on size.

2 Add the oranges to the other fruits with any juices, adding extra orange if necessary.

3 Leave to stand for 30 minutes. Serve the salad at room temperature, decorated with fresh mint leaves.

NUTRITIONAL VALUES

BREAKFAST CRUNCH

SERVES **4 – 6**

A delicious breakfast in a bowl, packed with goodness.

25 g sunflower seeds

25 g pine kernels

25 g sesame seeds

2 oranges

2 tbsp brown sugar

75 g dried figs, chopped

2 large bananas

600 ml low-fat Greek yoghurt

1 Using a dry frying pan, roast the sunflower seeds and pine kernels for 3 minutes over medium heat, then add the sesame seeds and roast for a further 3 minutes, stirring to give even browning. Remove the pan from the heat.

2 Coarsely grate the peel from 1 orange and add to the pan with the sugar and dried figs. Stir until well combined and cook for 2 minutes. Leave to cool.

3 Remove the peel and pith from the oranges and cut them into pieces. Slice the bananas and mix with the oranges and yoghurt, divide among four dishes and top each with the fig and seeds mixture. Serve at once.

NUTRITIONAL VALUES

LIGHT MEALS

HASH-BROWN POTATOES WITH BAKED BEANS

SERVES **6**

These golden potato cakes are served with a spicy bean dish, and are perfect for mopping up the delicious juices. Make the bean dish in advance and keep in the refrigerator until morning. Simply heat the beans in a pan over gentle heat.

FOR THE BAKED BEANS

190 g dried haricot beans, soaked overnight

170 ml vegetable stock

½ tsp dried mustard

1 onion, chopped

2 tbsp dark treacle

150 g tomatoes, peeled and chopped

1 tbsp tomato purée

1tbsp chopped fresh basil

freshly ground black pepper

FOR THE POTATO CAKES

450 g peeled, cubed potatoes

2 tbsp skimmed milk

1 onion, chopped

1 garlic clove, crushed

2 tsp olive oil

1 Drain the soaked beans and rinse well under cold water. Drain and put in a large saucepan with 300 ml of water. Bring the beans to a boil and boil rapidly for 10 minutes. Reduce the heat to a simmer, cover and cook for 1 hour or until the beans are cooked, topping up the water, if necessary. Drain the beans and return them to the pan. Stir in the vegetable stock, dried mustard, onion, treacle, tomatoes, tomato purée and basil. Season well and cook for 15 minutes or until the vegetables have cooked.

2 Make the potato cakes while the beans are cooking. Cook the potatoes in boiling water for 20 minutes or until just soft. Drain well and mash with the milk.

3 Add the onion and garlic, mixing well, and form into 12 equal-sized cakes. Brush a nonstick frying pan with the olive oil and warm over medium heat. Cook the potato cakes for 15 to 20 minutes, turning once, until golden brown. Serve piping hot with the baked beans.

NUTRITIONAL VALUES

STUFFED COURGETTES

SERVES 4

What better way to impress your guests than with these stuffed courgettes.

4 large courgettess

1 onion, peeled

1 red pepper, deseeded

1 green pepper, deseeded

4 tbsp olive oil

1 clove garlic, crushed

100 g cooked long-grain rice

100 g cooked chicken (optional)

2 tbsp cooked corn

$1/4$ tsp cumin

$1/2$ tsp gluten-free garam masala

freshly ground pepper

150 ml low-fat sour cream

1 tbsp chopped parsley

1 Wash the courgettess and cut a thin slice lengthways across the top of each. Scoop out the flesh and chop into small pieces. Cut a small slice off the bottom, if any of the courgettes are tipping over when laid flat.

2 Prepare the vegetables by dicing the onion and peppers. Heat the oil in a frying pan and cook the onion for 3 minutes. Then add the peppers and garlic. Cook for a further 3 minutes.

3 Add the rice and stir well. If you are using chicken, dice and add at this stage. Sprinkle in the corn and the seasonings over a low heat and mix for 1 minute.

4 Brush the courgette shells with oil and fill with the rice mixture. Pour the sour cream over and bake in the over for 20 minutes.

5 Sprinkle with chopped parsley. Oven temperature 180°C/gas mark 4.

NUTRITIONAL VALUES

STUFFED TOMATOES
SERVES **4**

Not only do these stuffed tomatoes look fantastic, but they're also healthy and quick and easy to cook.

4 large tomatoes

50 g long-grain rice, cooked

freshly ground black pepper

2 tbsp olive oil

1 large onion, peeled

1 green pepper, deseeded and sliced

1 chilli pepper, deseeded and sliced

1/2 tsp gluten-free curry powder (optional)

25 g almonds, chopped

1 tsp coriander or chopped parsley

50 g cooked minced beef, lamb or chicken

1 Remove the top of the tomatoes. Scoop out the centres into a bowl.

2 Add the cooked long-grain rice. Season well.

3 Heat the oil and fry the onion over a low heat for 3 minutes. Sprinkle with the curry powder and continue cooking for 2 minutes. Add the chopped almonds.

4 Finally sprinkle in the chopped coriander or parsley. Add the meat and mix well.

5 Fill each tomato with the rice mixture. Brush the tomatoes with oil. Then cook in the oven for about 15 minutes. Oven temperature 180°C/gas mark 4.

NUTRITIONAL VALUES

FRENCH BEANS AND NEW POTATOES IN PESTO

SERVES **4**

Although this dish takes advantage of the bounty of summer gardens, it can be made with potatoes and green beans that are available year-round, and pesto that is made in quantity during the summer and frozen in small batches.

450 g French beans, washed and trimmed

450 g tiny new potatoes, washed and cut in half

2 tbsp pine nuts or chopped walnuts

1 clove garlic, peeled

40 g fresh basil leaves

75 g Parmesan or Romano cheese, freshly grated if
   possible

5 tbsp olive oil

pinch of freshly ground black pepper

1 Boil the potatoes until tender, about 10 minutes. Boil the French beans until tender, 3–4 minutes. While the potatoes and beans are cooking, put the remaining ingredients in a food processor and process for about 10 seconds, until the basil is well chopped but the mixture is not turned into a paste.

2 Drain the potatoes and beans, toss with the pesto, and serve.

NUTRITIONAL VALUES

BEAN SPROUT AND RICE SALAD

SERVES **4**

This salad can be made in minutes, and has great flavour and texture to it.

approx 175 g can bean sprouts

1 tbsp olive oil

1 tbsp gluten-free soy sauce

1 small piece of root ginger,
 finely chopped

freshly ground black pepper

6 spring onions

100 g cooked long-grain rice

4 tbsp salad oil

2 tbsp lemon juice

1–2 tsp sugar

4 slices of Chinese leaves (Chinese
 cabbage or 'Bok Choy')

1 Drain the can of bean sprouts. Heat the olive oil in a small saucepan. Toss in the bean sprouts with the soy sauce and finely chopped ginger. Stir well. Cover and cook for 3 minutes on a low heat.

2 Turn the bean sprouts into a bowl and allow to cool. Season well.

3 Chop the spring onions into small pieces and add to the cooled shoots. Retain a few pieces for garnish.

4 Stir in the rice.

5 Mix the salad oil with the lemon juice in a screw-top jar.

6 Arrange the Chinese leaves in the bottom of the salad bowl. Shake the oil and lemon juice dressing and pour over the bean shoots and rice. Mix well and arrange in the salad bowl.

7 Garnish with a few rings of chopped spring onions.

NUTRITIONAL VALUES

RISOTTO WITH DRIED CEPS

SERVES **4 – 6**

In the autumn, Italians go mushroom hunting for porcini (ceps) which are very fleshy and can be served instead of a meat course.

50 g dried ceps

375 ml dry white wine

1 chicken stock cube or homemade chicken stock
   (see page 24)

1 small onion

60 ml olive oil

300 g Arborio (risotto) rice

100 g low-fat crème fraîche

3 tbsp freshly grated Parmesan cheese

salt substitute (see page 18) and freshly ground
   black pepper to taste

1 Put the dried ceps in a pot and cover them with the dry white wine. Pour the chicken stock over them and add 1 litre water.

2 Poach the ceps gently in the stock and wine until they are soft and swollen. Strain them carefully and reserve the poaching liquid. Wash the ceps once or twice more in fresh water: they can be gritty.

3 To remove grit from the poaching liquid, strain it too, through either muslin or a very fine strainer.

4 Boil the poaching liquid briskly. Your aim is to reduce its volume by about one third and consequently intensify its flavour.

5 As the mushroom stock boils, finely slice the onion, then soften it in a sturdy pan with the oil. Add the rice and toast it with the oil and onion.

6 Pour the mushroom liquid over the rice and let it cook until the liquid is almost absorbed. If this happens before the rice is cooked – about 15 minutes – add small amounts of water.

7 When the rice is cooked, stir in the low-fat crème fraîche and cheese; check the seasoning. Just before serving stir in the mushrooms.

NUTRITIONAL VALUES

LENTILS WITH MUSHROOMS AND ALMONDS

SERVES **4**

A delicious vegetarian light meal, this is an ideal midweek feast as a change from meat-based main dishes.

225 g green lentils, cooked

450 g button mushrooms, sliced

1 tsp ground mace

freshly ground black pepper

6 tbsp olive oil

75 g blanched almonds, split in half

225 g oyster mushrooms

4 tbsp snipped chives

NUTRITIONAL VALUES

1 The lentils should be freshly cooked, drained, and set aside in a covered pan so that they stay hot while the rest of the dish is prepared.

2 Mix the button mushrooms with the mace and plenty of seasoning. Heat 4 tablespoons of oil and stir-fry the mushrooms briskly until they begin to brown. When they give up their juices, continue stir-frying until all the liquid has evaporated and the mushrooms are greatly reduced in volume. At this stage they have a good, concentrated flavour; they should be dark in colour and most of the liquid in the pan should be the oil in which they have cooked.

3 Use a slotted spoon to remove the mushrooms from the pan and add them to the lentils. Cover and set aside. Stir-fry the almonds in the oil remaining in the pan until they are golden, then add them to the lentils. Fork the almonds and mushrooms into the lentils, then transfer the mixture to a serving dish or individual bowls.

4 Heat 2 tablespoons of oil in the pan and stir-fry the oyster mushrooms over fairly high heat for a minute or so – they should be very lightly cooked. If the mushrooms are overcooked they will collapse. Stir in the chives with a little seasoning, and spoon the mixture over the lentils, scraping any juices from the cooking pan. Serve at once.

MIXED PEPPER STIR-FRY WITH TOFU AND WALNUTS IN SWEET AND SOUR SAUCE

SERVES **4**

Crisp squares of golden fried tofu and roasted walnuts with multicoloured peppers served with traditional sweet and sour sauce and a bowl of rice.

350 g tofu, cut into bite-sized pieces

2–2¹/₂ fl oz olive oil for frying the tofu in the wok, more if you're using a flat frying pan

50 g walnut pieces

3–4 tbsp dark brown sugar

2 tbsp granulated sugar

6 tbsp hard cider vinegar or white wine vinegar

125 ml pineapple juice

2 tbsp gluten-free ketchup

1 tsp chopped ginger root

1 tbsp cornflour mixed with 5 tbsp cold water

2 tbsp oil for stir-frying or as needed

1 carrot, diagonally sliced

1 onion, cut lengthways into wedges or slices

1¹/₂ each: green, red, yellow, or orange peppers, cut into bite-sized pieces

3 to 4 tomatoes, cut into wedges

gluten-free soy sauce to taste

1 Dry the tofu pieces thoroughly on kitchen towels. Heat the oil in a wok and when very hot fry the tofu pieces over medium heat until golden brown on one side, then turn them and cook the other side until golden. Remove from the wok and place on paper towels to drain.

2 Deep-fry the walnuts in the wok for only a minute or so until golden brown (take care they do not burn, which they are apt to do quite easily). Remove with a slotted spoon and place on kitchen towels to drain. Remove the wok from the heat.

3 Make the sweet and sour sauce: combine the dark brown sugar in a saucepan with the granulated sugar, vinegar, pineapple juice, ketchup and ginger. Bring to a boil and cook for about 5 minutes or until slightly syrupy. Remove from the heat and stir in the cornflour mixed with water. Set aside.

4 Return the wok to the heat, you should have about 2.5 cm oil covering the bottom of the wok, remove or replenish oil as needed. Stir-fry the carrots for a minute or two then add the onions and stir-fry until both vegetables are lightly browned in spots, then add the peppers and tomatoes and stir-fry until all the vegetables, ensuring that they maintain their crispness

5 Add the tofu and the sweet and sour sauce, and cook for about 5 minutes until the tofu has heated through and the sauce has thickened. Season with gluten-free soy sauce to taste, sprinkle with the walnuts, and serve.

NUTRITIONAL VALUES

WINTER VEGETABLE CASSEROLE

SERVES **4 – 6**

The beauty of puy lentils, unlike other lentils, is that they keep their shape throughout the cooking process. Many people regard them as the best flavoured too.

1 tbsp olive oil

1 onion, peeled and cut into wedges

2–3 red serrano chillies, deseeded and chopped

1 tsp fennel seeds

½ tsp caraway seeds

2 medium carrots, peeled and sliced

1 acorn squash, peeled, deseeded and diced

175 g puy lentils, rinsed

300 g diced turnip

1 fennel bulb, trimmed and sliced

750 ml vegetable stock

1 tsp dried mixed herbs

few dashes Tabasco or hot sauce, to taste

freshly ground black pepper

2 tbsp chopped fresh parsley, to garnish

low-fat goat's cheese, crumbled, to serve

NUTRITIONAL VALUES

1 Preheat the cooker on high. Heat the oil in a frying pan and sauté the onion, garlic, chillies and fennel and caraway seeds for 3 minutes. Place in the cooking pot and add the rest of the ingredients except for the chopped parsley and cheese. Mix well.

2 Cook on high for 3–4 hours. Serve sprinkled with the chopped parsley and crumbled goat's cheese.

SPICED RICE SALAD

SERVES **4**

This is ideal for those who want their salads with a bit more bite to them. It is a great summer dish, and also good as a side for a main meal.

220 g rice

1 tsp gluten-free garam masala

1 tsp tumeric

1 bay leaf

1 tbsp olive oil

1 clove garlic, minced

1 onion, peeled and diced

50 g golden raisins

1 green pepper, deseeded, blanched and diced

GARNISH

6 tbsp low-fat yoghurt

2 shallots, washed

1 Cook the rice in boiling water with the gluten-free garam masala, tumeric and bay leaf for about 15 minutes until tender.

2 Meanwhile heat the oil and gently sweat the garlic and onion without browning for 5 minutes.

3 Add the garlic and onion to the rice when it is cooked and allow it to cool.

4 Stir in the golden raisins and pepper.

5 Garnish with chopped shallots. Stir in yoghurt before serving.

NUTRITIONAL VALUES

WALDORF RICE SALAD

A lovely crisp salad, which is full of fantastic colour.

229 g long-grain rice

1 small onion, peeled and minced

6 sticks celery, washed

4 shallots, washed and chopped

50 g walnuts, chopped

1 red apple

1 green apple

150 g low-fat mayonnaise

1 tbsp fresh parsley

juice of 1 lemon

NUTRITIONAL VALUES

1 Cook the rice until fluffy, forking from time to time to separate the grains. Allow to cool.

2 Add the minced onion to the rice and mix well.

3 Remove the strings from the celery sticks and mince. Add to the rice.

4 Add the chopped shallots and walnuts to the rice and mix well.

5 Chop part of both apples into small cubes, sprinkle with lemon juice and mix with the rice salad, mayonnaise and parsley.

6 Decorate with remaining apple slices and walnut halves.

MIXED BEAN CHILLI

SERVES **4**

Chilli con carne has always been a warming favourite, and this recipe without the 'carne' is no exception. Packed with vegetables and beans, it is a fully satisfying meal.

450 g canned beans such as borlotti, red kidney, black-eyed, and pinto beans, drained

400 g can chopped tomatoes

1 tbsp gluten-free tomato purée

1 onion, halved and sliced

75 g cubed potatoes

1 green pepper, deseeded and chopped

110 g halved baby corn cobs

2 green chillies, deseeded and chopped

1 tsp chilli powder

2 cloves garlic, crushed

125 ml vegetable stock

chopped fresh parsley, to garnish

1 Place all of the ingredients except the garnish in a large saucepan and bring to a boil. Reduce the heat, cover the pan, and simmer for 45 minutes, or until all of the vegetables are cooked and the juices have thickened slightly. Stir the chilli occasionally while cooking.

2 Garnish with parsley and serve with brown rice or baked potatoes.

NUTRITIONAL VALUES

SUMMER COUSCOUS SALAD

SERVES **6**

You can serve couscous cold as a salad, with just toasted pine nuts and a fruity olive oil dressing. This is more of a mixed vegetable salad, spiced with roasted peppers and chillies.

2 red peppers

3–4 chillies, according to taste

300 g couscous

75 g pine nuts, toasted

100 g finely sliced button mushrooms

1 small courgette, chopped finely

3 tbsp vinaigrette or extra-virgin olive oil

freshly ground black pepper

1 tbsp freshly chopped parsley

1 avocado, sliced and tossed in lemon juice

1 Preheat an oven to 200°C/gas mark 6. Place the peppers and chillies on a baking tray and roast in the oven for 30–40 minutes, turning once during cooking. The chillies may only take 20 minutes to blacken and should be removed as soon as they are ready. Cover the hot peppers with a damp tea towel and leave until cool. Remove the skins by peeling from the flower end, then discard the core and seeds and chop the flesh.

2 Cover the couscous with boiling water and allow it to stand for at least 20 minutes; add a little more water if it seems dry, but do not drown the grains. Add the roasted peppers and all the remaining ingredients and toss thoroughly. Transfer to a bowl or platter and garnish with the avocado just before serving.

NUTRITIONAL VALUES

RICE AND PISTACHIO SALAD

SERVES **4 – 6**

Wild rice is available either by itself or in a mix with instant white rice. The latter makes an ideal base for this salad, which is mixed with raisins and pistachios and thickened with a honey dressing.

250 g brown and white rice mix

50 g raisins

50 g pistachios, shelled

4 spring onions, trimmed and sliced

4 tomatoes, chopped

DRESSING

50 ml clear honey

1 tbsp cider vinegar

grated rind and juice of 1 lemon

2 tbsp olive oil

freshly ground black pepper

1 tbsp freshly chopped chives

1   Bring the rices to the boil in plenty of water, then cover and simmer for 20 minutes. While the rice is cooking, whisk all the ingredients for the dressing together and season to taste. Drain the rice thoroughly then add the dressing and toss it with the grains. Transfer the rice to a bowl and allow it to cool completely.

2   Add the remaining ingredients to the salad and stir them carefully into the rice. Season to taste with extra pepper before serving.

NUTRITIONAL VALUES

WICKLOW PANCAKES

SERVES **4**

This is a simple recipe that uses only a few basic ingredients.

450 g onions

675 g potatoes, sliced

6 tbsp olive oil

salt substitute (see page 18) and freshly ground
   black pepper

6 eggs

parsley

NUTRITIONAL VALUES

1 Peel and slice the onions and potatoes and stew in
the olive oil until they are very well cooked – do
try not to brown either the onions or the potatoes.
Drain off the excess oil, season to taste.

2 Whisk the eggs in a large bowl, then add the
potato and onion mixture, along with some
chopped parsley. Put a little oil in a frying
pan and pour some of the mixture in
until it is nearly 2.5 cm thick.

3 Cook over a moderate heat until
reasonably firm, then turn over
with the help of a dinner plate.
Cook for a few minutes and turn
out.

4 Cut into wedges and eat hot or
cold.

RED PEPPER, CORN AND CHEESE POLENTA

SERVES **4**

Instant polenta may not be as flavourful as the original long-cooking variety, but is very convenient, and just as sumptuous.

2 red peppers, diced

1 onion, chopped

5 cloves garlic, chopped

4 tbsp extra-virgin olive oil

375 ml instant or ordinary long-cooking polenta

1 litre boiling water

3–5 small sprigs fresh rosemary, stems removed, the leaves chopped (2–3 tsp)

250 g cooked corn kernels

400 g can chopped tomatoes, including the juices, or about 8 ripe flavourful fresh tomatoes, diced

750 g grated Jarlsburg or Gruyère cheese

6 tbsp grated parmesan cheese, or to taste

freshly ground black pepper to taste

NUTRITIONAL VALUES

1 Lightly sauté the peppers, onion, and garlic in the olive oil until softened, then stir in the polenta grains and cook them lightly in the olive oil, allowing them to absorb the flavour of the oil, and cook slightly.

2 Stir in the water, about a third at a time, letting it cook and absorb between additions, and when about half the water has been absorbed stir in the rosemary, corn and tomatoes, then continue with the water until it reaches a soft, thick consistency. This will take 5 to 8 minutes if using instant polenta, and about 30 minutes if using the long-cooking variety.

3 Stir in the cheeses and hot sauce to taste, and serve in bowls, with extra cheese on the side if wished.

ROASTED SWEET POTATOES WITH RED PEPPER-LIME BUTTER

SERVES **4**

With its wonderful colour and flavour, a sweet potato is a great alternative to a jacket potato. This recipe contains mild chilli which will complement the sweet potato beautifully.

4 sweet potatoes, preferably orange-fleshed

1 red pepper, roasted, peeled and diced

3–4 cloves garlic, chopped

1–2 tbsp olive oil

1 tsp mild chili powder

¼ tsp cumin, or more to taste

8 tbsp butter, at room temperature or softened

juice of ½ lime, or to taste

1 Preheat the oven to 190°C/gas mark 5.

2 Roast the sweet potatoes in the oven, in their skins, for about 40 minutes or until they are just tender. Alternatively, microwave them for about 5 minutes on high, then transfer them to the oven and roast at 200°C/gas mark 6 for about 10 minutes.

3 Meanwhile, make the red pepper-lime butter. Mix the pepper with the garlic, olive oil, chilli powder, and cumin until it forms a thick mixture, then work in the soft butter. Taste for seasoning, then add lime juice as desired.

4 Serve this pepper butter spooned into each potato, or serve the sweet potatoes cut into thick slices with a piece of the butter on top.

NUTRITIONAL VALUES

PINEAPPLE RICE

SERVES 4 – 6

A 'show-off' dish that is quite easy to make but always impressive to present. Although the pineapple also adds flavour to the rice, there is scarcely any point attempting it just with pineapple pieces – appearance is everything.

1 pineapple

4 tbsp peanut or corn oil

550 g cooked rice

75 g finely diced ham

$1/2$ tbsp chopped garlic

50 g raisins

2 tbsp chicken stock

2 tsp gluten-free curry powder

1 tsp sugar

$1/4$ tsp ground white pepper

1 Cut one side off the pineapple lengthways to expose the inside. Carefully remove the inside fruits and cut into small dice. Reserve the outside of the pineapple.

2 Heat the oil in a pan or wok, add the ham and garlic, stir-fry, then add 75 g of the diced pineapple and all the rest of the ingredients. Mix well. Spoon into the empty pineapple, cover with the pineapple lid and bake in a preheated 140°C/gas mark 1 oven for 30 minutes.

NUTRITIONAL VALUES

RISOTTO WITH SQUASH

SERVES **4**

Squash combines with tomatoes in this buttery risotto. Serve this as an unusual accompaniment to a casserole, or as a delicious light meal.

1.1 litres vegetable stock

3 tbsp olive oil

2 medium red onions, finely chopped

2 garlic cloves, crushed

450 g butternut squash fresh, diced

400 g arborio rice

freshly ground black pepper

150 ml dry white wine

400 g can chopped tomatoes

2 tbsp chopped fresh parsley

NUTRITIONAL VALUES

1 Pour the stock into a saucepan and bring to a boil. Reduce the heat to a gentle simmer.

2 Meanwhile, heat the oil and gently fry the onion, garlic, and squash for 7–8 minutes until just softening. Add the rice and cook, stirring, for 2 minutes until well mixed. Season well.

3 Add the wine and chopped tomatoes and cook gently, stirring, until absorbed. Add the stock, ladle-by-ladle, until the liquid is absorbed and the rice is thick, creamy and tender. Keep the heat moderate. This will take about 25 minutes.

4 Adjust seasoning if necessary. Serve sprinkled with chopped parsley.

SICILIAN ARTICHOKE RISOTTO

SERVES **4**

This gluten-free risotto contains good levels of antioxidants but also has a high GI value, so try to eat low GI foods on the days you make this dish.

5 tbsp coarsely chopped bacon

1 onion

1 clove garlic

$\frac{1}{2}$ stick celery

1 bunch parsley

olive oil

75 g peeled, deseeded, chopped tomato

freshly ground black pepper

250 g artichoke hearts packed in water, drained

625 ml cold water

150 g rice

60 g grated pecorino cheese

1 Chop together the bacon, onion, garlic, celery and parsley and fry in a few tablespoons oil. Then add the tomato, season with pepper and cook gently for 10 minutes.

2 Add the artichoke hearts and cold water and cook for 10 minutes longer. Bring to a boil, add the rice and cook for 20 minutes or until just tender. Stir in the grated pecorino cheese to serve.

NUTRITIONAL VALUES

CHINESE NOODLES

SERVES **4**

This is a really quick and easy dish for a speedy lunch or supper. Use rice noodles for a Chinese flavour or pasta ribbons if preferred, but these will require cooking for 8–10 minutes.

250 g thin egg or rice noodles

85 ml vegetable stock

2 cloves garlic, crushed

1 red onion, halved and sliced

2.5 cm piece of ginger root, grated

1 red chilli, chopped

2 carrots, cut into strips

100 g snow peas

1 courgette, sliced

1 celery stick, sliced

1 tsp curry powder

3 tbsp dark gluten-free soy sauce

3 tbsp plum sauce

1 tsp fennel seeds

chopped fresh parsley or fennel leaves, to garnish

NUTRITIONAL VALUES

1 Cook the noodles in boiling water for 3 minutes. Drain and reserve.

2 Meanwhile, heat the stock in a non-stick wok or frying pan and cook the vegetables and spices for 3 to 4 minutes, stirring constantly.

3 Add the drained noodles to the pan with the soy and plum sauces and the fennel seeds. Cook for 2 to 3 minutes, tossing well and serve garnished with parsley or fennel leaves.

FIVE-SPICE PORK WITH NOODLES

SERVES **4**

This can also be made with skinless chicken breasts or a vegetarian substitute such as bean curd.

450 g lean, boneless pork, thinly sliced

¹/₂ tsp five-spice powder

salt substitute (see page 18) and freshly ground black
    pepper

2 spring onions, finely chopped

1 clove garlic, crushed

225 g rice noodles

3 tbsp peanut oil

225 g tinned bamboo shoots

225 g mange tout, trimmed

3 tbsp Japanese gluten-free soy sauce or Chinese light
    gluten-free soy sauce

2 tbsp toasted sesame seeds

1   Mix the pork with the five-spice powder, seasoning, spring onions and garlic. Cover, refrigerate, and leave to marinate for two hours.

2   Place the noodles in a pan and pour over boiling water to cover. Bring back to the boil and cook for 2 minutes, then drain and rinse under cold water. Leave to drain.

3   In a wok or frying pan, heat the oil and stir-fry the pork until well browned. Add the sliced bamboo shoots and peas, and stir-fry for 3–4 minutes, or until the vegetables are cooked. Push the mixture to one side of the wok and add the noodles. Stir-fry the noodles for 2 minutes to heat through, then stir in the reserved mixture, soy sauce and sesame seeds. Stir-fry for 1 minute before serving.

NUTRITIONAL VALUES

SWEETCORN, CHICKEN AND PRAWN CHOWDER

SERVES **4 – 6**

The word 'chowder' derives from the French Canadian cooking utensil chaudière. Originally Newfoundland fishermen made a stew of cod and potatoes, but the recipe developed to include clams, scallops and salmon.

2 tbsp olive oil

2 medium onions, finely chopped

2 medium potatoes, peeled and diced

2 pinches grated nutmeg

750 ml chicken stock

salt substitute (see page 18) and freshly ground
    black pepper

50 g streaky smoked bacon, derinded and
    chopped

1 boneless chicken breast, approx. 150 g, skinned
    and sliced in strips

1 small can, approx. 225 g, gluten-free sweetcorn
    kernels, drained

125 g peeled prawns (or 4 scallops, chopped)

300 ml milk

4 tbsp fromage frais

freshly chopped chervil, to garnish

1 Heat the oil in a large saucepan and cook the onions for 10 minutes, or until softened, but not browned. Add the diced potato and nutmeg and cook for a further 5 minutes. Stir in the stock, cover, and simmer for 15 minutes. Purée in a liquidizer. Season to taste.

2 Fry the bacon in its own fat until well browned. Add the chicken and cook for a further 2 minutes. Stir in the sweetcorn kernels, and prawns or scallops. Add the puréed stock mixture and blend in the milk. Simmer gently for 10 minutes or until the chicken is tender. Season to taste.

3 Serve in deep bowls, garnished with a swirl of fromage frais and a dusting of chervil. Accompany with gluten-free crusty brown bread.

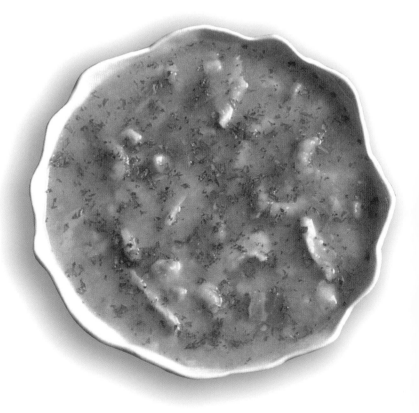

NUTRITIONAL VALUES

AVOCADO AND CHICKEN SALAD

SERVES **4**

This is a quick, yet delicious, way of using up any left-over cooked chicken – a perfect summer lunch. Try ringing the changes with mango instead of avocado.

450 g cooked chicken meat, in small chunks

2 ripe avocados

1 tbsp lemon juice

4 tomatoes, skinned

2 spring onions, chopped

2 tbsp chopped parsley

50 g cashew nuts, toasted

GARLIC VINAIGRETTE

3 tbsp groundnut oil

1 tbsp white wine vinegar

1 tbsp Dijon mustard

1 clove garlic, minced

$1/2$ tsp caster sugar

salt substitute (see page 18) and freshly
   ground black pepper

GARNISH

1 tbsp chopped parsley

1 Split the avocado in half, remove the stone (pit) and skin and cut into neat slices. Brush with the lemon juice to prevent discolouration.

2 Slice each tomato and arrange alternately with the avocado around the outer edge of a flat serving plate, as shown.

3 Mix the chicken with the spring onions, parsley, and nuts. Whisk together the Garlic Vinaigrette ingredients. There should be enough to coat the chicken well.

4 Pile the mixture in the centre of the plate. Brush any remaining dressing over the avocado and tomato slices. Garnish with a sprinkling of parsley.

NUTRITIONAL VALUES

STIR-FRY CHICKEN AND SPINACH SALAD

SERVES **4**

This is a simple yet tasty salad topped with stir-fry chicken, onions and garlic.

175 g fresh young spinach leaves

6 small spring onions, trimmed and sliced

2 tbsp toasted hazelnuts, chopped

2 small courgettes, thinly sliced

2 boneless chicken breasts, skinned,
    approx. 150 g each

6 tbsp light olive oil

1 small onion, finely chopped

1 clove garlic, finely chopped

2 tbsp white wine vinegar

salt substitute (see page 18) and freshly ground
    black pepper

1 tbsp fresh tarragon, chopped, or 1 tsp dried

small sweet red pepper, deseeded and diced, to
    garnish

1 Rinse and lightly shake the spinach leaves. Tear into pieces and place in a bowl or on individual serving plates. Sprinkle on the spring onions, hazelnuts and courgettes.

2 Cut the chicken into thin strips. Heat two thirds of the oil in a large, shallow pan and briskly stir-fry the chicken with the onion and garlic until just tender.

3 Stir in the remaining olive oil, wine vinegar, salt and pepper, and tarragon. Allow to cook for a further minute. Spoon the hot chicken and dressing over the salad ingredients.

4 Sprinkle with the diced sweet red pepper and serve immediately.

NUTRITIONAL VALUES

STARTERS

THAI HOT AND SOUR

SERVES **4**

This is one of the most exquisite dishes of Thai cuisine. The stock is a myriad of texture and flavours – sour lime leaves and lemon grass, spicy ginger, chillies and sweet seafood.

1 tbsp olive oil

2 cloves garlic, finely chopped

2 shallot, finely chopped

1 cm piece root ginger, sliced thin

4–5 small red chillies, chopped

1.4 litres light chicken stock (see page 24)

3 Kaffir lime leaves, sliced

10 cm piece lemon grass, chopped

200 g rice vermicelli

20 large cooked prawns, shelled and
    deveined

6 tbsp fish sauce

6 tbsp fresh lemon or lime juice

2 tbsp granulated brown sugar

16 tinned straw mushrooms

fresh coriander leaves

1   Heat the oil in a pan. When hot, stir-fry the garlic, shallots, ginger and chillies for 1 minute. Pour in the stock, then add the lime leaves and lemon grass. Bring to the boil and simmer for 5 minutes.

2   Meanwhile, soak the noodles for 3 minutes in warm water, drain and rinse under cold water. Drain before dividing the noodles among four bowls. Add the prawns, fish sauce, lemon juice, sugar and mushrooms to the stock and simmer for 3 minutes. Pour over the noodles and sprinkle with coriander.

NUTRITIONAL VALUES

BUCKWHEAT AND MUSHROOM SOUP

SERVES **6**

Buckwheat has a strong, slightly sweet and fragrantly nutty flavour. It is often the principal ingredient of simple rustic soups and stews, but in this more luxurious recipe, it blends with fresh and dried mushrooms to produce a very creamy soup. Only a little buckwheat is required to achieve a subtle flavouring.

25 g dried cep mushrooms

250 ml sherry

2 tbsp olive oil

1 onion, finely chopped

2 celery sticks, finely chopped

2 slices sweet cure bacon, finely chopped

250 g mushrooms, roughly chopped

2 plump garlic cloves, finely sliced

45 g raw buckwheat

1.2 litres well-flavoured vegetable stock (see page 23)

salt substitute (see page 18) and freshly ground
    black pepper

grated fresh nutmeg

300 ml milk

low-fat crème fraîche and paprika, to garnish

1 Soak the ceps in the sherry for at least 30 minutes before starting the soup. Heat the oil, then add the onion, celery and bacon, and cook slowly for about 5 minutes until the vegetables have softened but not browned.

2 Add the chopped mushrooms and garlic and cook slowly for a further 2–3 minutes until the juices start to run from the mushrooms. Add the ceps and the sherry, then stir in the buckwheat and pour in the stock.

3 Bring the soup slowly to the boil, stirring up any sediment from the bottom of the pan. Season lightly with the salt substitute, pepper and grated nutmeg then cover the pan and gently simmer the soup for 40 minutes.

4 Allow the soup to cool slightly then purée until smooth in a blender. Rinse the pan and return the soup to it with the milk. Reheat, then season to taste. Garnish with a swirl of créme fraîche and a little paprika before serving in warmed soup bowls with warm crusty bread.

NUTRITIONAL VALUES

CHINESE CHICKEN AND CORN SOUP

SERVES **6**

This Chinese soup is appreciated around the world, and should not be reserved just for Oriental meals. The delicate flavours and subtle spicing make it an approachable and suitably light starter for entertaining.

1.4 litres chicken stock (see page 24)

2 boneless skinless chicken breasts

1 small onion, roughly chopped

1 carrot, roughly chopped

1 celery stick, roughly chopped

2.5 cm piece fresh ginger root, peeled and sliced

bouquet garni (parsley stems, leek greens, and bay leaf)

4 ears of corn, 375 g thawed frozen or gluten-free canned corn kernels

3 tbsp cornflour

8 spring onions

white pepper

2 egg whites, beaten with 3 tbsp water

60 g cooked ham, cut into matchstick strips

1 Put the stock in a large saucepan with the chicken, onion, carrot, celery, ginger and bouquet garni. Bring to the boil over medium–high heat, skimming off any foam as it rises to the surface. Reduce the heat to medium–low and simmer, partially covered, for 30–40 minutes, or until the chicken is very tender. Strain the stock, remove the chicken and discard the vegetables. Shred the chicken.

2 Cut the kernels from the corn, without cutting down to the cob. With the back of a knife, scrape the cobs to extract the milky liquid from the base of kernels.

3 Combine the strained stock, half the spring onions, and the corn kernels and their liquid, if available, in the saucepan, and season with white pepper. Bring to the boil slowly over medium heat and boil gently for 5 minutes.

4 Stir the cornflour into 3 tablespoons cold water until dissolved and pour into the soup, stirring constantly. Cook, stirring, until the soup thickens, about 5 minutes. Slowly pour the egg whites into the soup while stirring vigorously. Add the ham and shredded chicken, and heat through, 1–2 minutes. Ladle into warm bowls and garnish with the remaining spring onions.

NUTRITIONAL VALUES

CHILLED GREEN PEA SOUP

SERVES 6

This soup is a stunning bright green colour. It is simple to make and quite tasty using frozen peas, but if you are able to find fresh-picked young garden peas, you are in for a real gourmet treat.

1 tbsp olive oil

4 shallots, finely chopped

900 g shelled fresh peas or thawed frozen peas

1 litre water

freshly ground black pepper

80 ml low-fat cream

2 tbsp chopped fresh mint

12–18 small snow peas, blanched and chilled, for garnishing

1 Warm the oil in a large saucepan over medium-low heat. Add the shallots and cook, stirring occasionally, until they begin to soften, about 5 minutes.

2 Add the peas and water. Season with a little pepper. Simmer covered, stirring occasionally, until the vegetables are tender, about 12 minutes for frozen or young fresh peas, or up to 18 minutes for large or older peas.

3 Transfer the solids to a blender or a food processor fitted with a steel blade. Add some of the cooking liquid and purée until smooth, working in batches if necessary. Strain into a bowl with the remaining cooking liquid, allow to stand until cool, cover and refrigerate until cold.

4 Using an electric mixer or whisk, whip the cream in a chilled bowl until soft peaks form. Stir in the mint.

5 Thin the soup with a little cold water, if needed, and adjust the seasoning. Ladle into chilled soup plates and garnish each with a dollop of low-fat cream and 2 or 3 snow peas.

NUTRITIONAL VALUES

ICED TOMATO AND ORANGE SOUP

SERVES **4**

This lean, flavourful soup depends on ripe tomatoes. Use seasonal sun-ripened tomatoes at their peak – plum tomatoes are best.

2 tsp olive oil

1 large sweet onion, chopped

1 medium carrot, chopped

1 kg ripe tomatoes, cored and quartered

1 orange (unwashed or scrubbed), thinly
    sliced

bouquet garni (thyme and marjoram sprigs
    and bay leaf)

250 ml water

salt substitute (see page 18) and freshly
    ground black pepper

125 ml fresh orange juice

mint sprigs, for garnishing

1 Heat the olive oil in a large non-reactive saucepan or flameproof casserole over medium heat. Add the onion and carrot, and cook for 4–5 minutes, stirring occasionally, until the onion is just softened.

2 Add the tomatoes, orange and bouquet garni. Reduce the heat to medium-low, cover, and simmer for about 40 minutes, stirring once or twice, until the vegetables are very soft.

3 Work the tomato mixture through a food mill fitted with a fine blade set over a bowl. Add the orange juice and season to taste with salt and pepper. Strain the soup, allow to cool, cover and refrigerate until cold. Serve in glasses, with ice cubes if you like and garnish with mint sprigs.

NUTRITIONAL VALUES

GAZPACHO SORBET

SERVES **6**

This piquant sorbet makes an unusual starter, excellent to serve while waiting for your drumsticks to cook on the barbecue. Serve in glasses, garnished with finely diced salad vegetables such as peppers, cucumber and spring onions. The flavour will become much stronger if frozen.

1 tbsp caster sugar

125 ml water

425 ml tomato juice

1–2 tbsp tomato purée

2 spring onions, trimmed and chopped

1/2 green pepper, seeds removed and chopped

1 green chilli, seeds removed and chopped

1 small clove garlic

1 tbsp lemon juice

dash of Worcestershire sauce

freshly ground black pepper

1 Use the sugar and water to make a sugar syrup. Allow to cool completely.

2 Blend all the remaining ingredients together into a smooth purée in a liquidizer or food processor. Press the purée through a sieve, using the back of a ladle to force it through; this will give a very smooth base for the sorbet.

3 Combine the sugar syrup with the sieved tomato mixture, season well, then pour into the ice-cream machine. Freeze-churn until ready to serve.

NUTRITIONAL VALUES

CREAMY PURÉE OF WHITE BEANS AND PORCINI

SERVES **4 – 6**

Humble beans puréed with luxurious wild mushrooms create this classic soup, which is popular in the southwest of France. The soup is sometimes served with a scattering of grated prosciutto, a shaving of truffle, a drizzle of truffle oil, or a scattering of diced foie gras.

450 g cooked white beans (such as cannellini)

2.5 litres stock, preferably ham

50 g diced ham or bacon (such as pancetta or prosciutto)

1 carrot, diced

1 baking potato, diced

2–3 tsp fresh thyme leaves

5 garlic cloves, roughly chopped

50 g dried mushrooms (such as porcini)

1 cup water

3 tbsp brandy

salt substitute (see page 18) and freshly ground black pepper

2 tbsp low-fat crème fraîche

1 In a saucepan, combine the beans with the stock, ham or bacon, carrot, potato, half the thyme and the garlic. Bring to the boil, then reduce the heat to low, and simmer for about 30 minutes, until the vegetables are tender and cooked through.

2 Meanwhile, place the mushrooms with the water and brandy in a saucepan. Gradually bring to the boil, then reduce the heat, and simmer for about 15 minutes until the mushrooms are tender.

3 Remove the mushrooms from the liquid, chop roughly and add them to the soup. Strain the liquid discarding the gritty bits, and add the strained liquid to the soup.

4 Mix the soup in the blender or food processor until smooth. Taste for seasoning, then stir in the créme fraîche. Serve immediately in warmed bowls, garnished with thyme.

NUTRITIONAL VALUES

GINGERED CHESTNUT SOUP

SERVES **6**

Ginger has been used in remedies across the globe, and is said to be beneficial in the treatment of all sorts of illnesses.

2 tbsp olive oil

1 large onion, chopped

225 g carrots, scraped and chopped (about 3 or 4 carrots)

45 g chopped fresh ginger

450 g chestnuts, roasted, shelled and peeled

1 bay leaf

freshly ground white pepper to taste

1 litre chicken stock (see page 24)

250 ml dry white wine

40 ml fresh lemon juice

low-fat sour cream for garnish

1   Heat the oil in a large saucepan over medium heat. Add the onion, carrots and ginger and sauté gently for 10 minutes.

2   Add the chestnuts, bay leaf, and white pepper and stock. Bring the mixture to the boil, then cover, lower the heat, and simmer for 45 minutes. Remove the bay leaf. Purée the mixture in batches in a blender or food processor fitted with a steel blade. Add the wine and lemon juice. (The soup can be prepared in advance to this point and refrigerated.)

3   Rinse the saucepan thoroughly return the puréed soup to it and heat slowly stirring frequently to prevent sticking. You may add more stock if the soup is too thick for your taste, but remember that it will thin a little as it heats.

4   Serve garnished with a dollop of low-fat sour cream.

NUTRITIONAL VALUES

ROASTED ACORN SOUP WITH CUCUMBER SALSA

SERVES **4**

This creamy, nutty-flavoured soup is further enhanced by a subtly spicy, crunchy cucumber salsa.

1 acorn squash (weighing about 600 g) quartered

freshly grated nutmeg

olive oil

1 large onion, chopped fine

2 slices bacon, rinded and chopped

2 large carrots, sliced

4–5 rocket, shredded fine, or 3 bay leaves

1 litre well-flavoured vegetable stock (see page 23)

freshly ground black pepper

250 ml milk

FOR THE SALSA

1 tbsp coriander seeds

$1/2$ medium cucumber, deseeded and diced

1 mild green chilli, deseeded and chopped very fine

1 small red onion, chopped fine

1 fresh tomato, deseeded and chopped

1 garlic clove, chopped fine

2.5 cm piece fresh ginger root, shredded

NUTRITIONAL VALUES

1 Preheat a 220°C/gas mark 7 oven. Scrape the seeds out of the squash, then arrange the pieces in a roasting pan, and season lightly with nutmeg. Drizzle with a little olive oil, then roast the squash for 45 minutes, or until tender. Then leave to cool.

2 Meanwhile, cook the onion, bacon and carrots with 1 tablespoon of olive oil in a covered pan for 4–5 minutes, until the vegetables are tender. Scoop the roasted squash from the skin, chop it roughly, then add it to the pan with the lovage or bay and stock. Season lightly with pepper, then bring to the boil. Cover the pan and simmer for 30 minutes.

3 Meanwhile, prepare the salsa. Heat a small frying pan over medium heat until hot, then add the coriander seeds and fry for about 1 minute, until roasted and fragrant. Crush the seeds lightly using a pestle and mortar, or use the end of a rolling pin. Add all the other salsa ingredients except the ginger. Finally, gather up the ginger shreds in your hands and squeeze just the juice into the mixture. Leave to stand for about 30 minutes, to allow the flavours to blend.

4 Cool the soup slightly, then blend until smooth in a blender or food processor, adding the milk. Season to taste and reheat if necessary. Serve the soup with a generous spoonful of salsa in each portion.

BLUEBERRY VICHYSSOISE

SERVES **4**

This has a cool and slightly fruity flavour that is ideal as a starter or a cool snack in the summer. It is delicious served with thinly sliced gluten-free bread.

5 new potatoes, washed in cold water

4–5 spring onions, white part only

750 ml chicken stock (see page 24)

120 ml low-fat soured cream

150 g blueberries

120 ml milk

1 Cut washed potatoes into quarters.

2 Cut spring onions into 1 cm pieces.

3 In a 4 litre pan, heat chicken stock, potatoes, and spring onions to the boil. Lower to a simmer.

4 Cook for about 30 minutes, until potatoes are soft.

5 Sieve stock mixture and return to pan; discard pulp left in sieve. Bring back to a simmer over a low heat.

6 Whisk in the low-fat soured cream. Add ³/₄ of the berries and cook on low heat until the first berries split. Set aside remaining berries.

7 Remove from heat and chill overnight.

8 With a fork, mash the blueberry mixture and thin with the milk until desired consistency.

9 Garnish with the remainder of the uncooked berries.

NUTRITIONAL VALUES

COCONUT-PRAWN SOUP

SERVES **4 – 6**

Creates a warm and creamy seafood soup with a hint of the caribbean, and makes a wonderful accompaniment to any meal.

1 litre coconut milk, made from 2 fresh coconuts (canned unsweetened coconut milk may be substituted)

2 medium-size onions, chopped

1 garlic clove, crushed

10 black peppercorns

3 coriander seeds

zest of 1 lemon, removed with a vegetable peeler or sharp knife

1 tsp cumin seeds

3 parsley sprigs

1 or 2 hot fresh chillies (to taste), deseeded and coarsely chopped

450 g raw shrimps, shelled, deveined, and chopped

1 tsp sugar

40 ml fresh lemon juice

salt substitute (see page 18) to taste

4–6 peeled cooked prawns for garnish (optional)

15 g grated fresh coconut for garnish (optional)

1 Place the coconut milk and onions in a medium-size saucepan and bring to the boil. Place the garlic, peppercorns, coriander seeds, lemon zest, cumin seeds, parsley and chillies in a spice bag or a piece of muslin, tied shut, and add it to the saucepan. Cover, lower the heat and simmer for 25 minutes.

2 Add the prawns, sugar, lemon juice and salt substitute to taste and simmer for 5 minutes more. Remove the spice bag. Serve hot, garnished with whole prawns and grated coconut if desired.

NUTRITIONAL VALUES

PEAR AND GRAPE SALAD

SERVES **4**

A delicious combination of tastes and textures. This salad makes an equally good appetizer or side dish to main dishes based on grains or beans.

2 little gem lettuces, or ½ head Iceberg lettuce, torn into bite-sized pieces

1 head chicory, trimmed and sliced

2 large ripe dessert pears, peeled and sliced

juice of ½ lemon

100 g dessert grapes, preferably black, halved and deseeded

125 g low-fat soured cream

75 g low-fat cream cheese

1–2 cloves garlic, crushed

freshly ground black pepper

paprika

NUTRITIONAL VALUES

1 Mix together the lettuce and chicory and arrange in a salad bowl or on individual plates. Toss the pears in the lemon juice and arrange the pieces over the lettuce, then add the grapes.

2 Blend together the low-fat soured cream and low-fat cream cheese, add the garlic, and season well with pepper. Spoon the dressing into the centre of the salad, garnish with paprika, then serve with fresh, crusty, gluten-free wholewheat bread.

ASPARAGUS WITH RED PEPPER SAUCE

SERVES **4**

This bright red pepper sauce looks terrific spooned over asparagus spears. If you don't want to make a spicy sauce, either reduce the amount of chilli sauce added, or omit it altogether.

450 g asparagus spears, trimmed

grated zest of 1 lemon

parsley sprigs to garnish

FOR THE SAUCE

3 red peppers, halved and deseeded

475 ml vegetable stock

1 tsp gluten-free chilli sauce

juice of 1 lemon

1 garlic clove, crushed

1   To make the sauce, cook the peppers under a hot grill, skin side uppermost for 5 minutes until the skin begins to blacken and blister. Transfer the peppers to a plastic bag using tongs, seal, and leave for 20 minutes. Peel the skin from the red peppers and discard.

2   Roughly chop the peppers and put them in a saucepan with the stock, chilli sauce, lemon juice and garlic.

3   Cook over a gentle heat for 20 minutes or until the peppers are tender. Transfer the sauce to a food processor and blend for 10 seconds. Return the purée to the saucepan and heat through gently.

4   Meanwhile, tie the asparagus spears into four equal bundles. Stand upright in a steamer or saucepan filled with boiling water and cook for 10–15 minutes until tender. Remove the asparagus from the pan and untie the bundles. Arrange on four serving plates and spoon the sauce over the top. Sprinkle the lemon zest on top, garnish with parsley and serve.

NUTRITIONAL VALUES

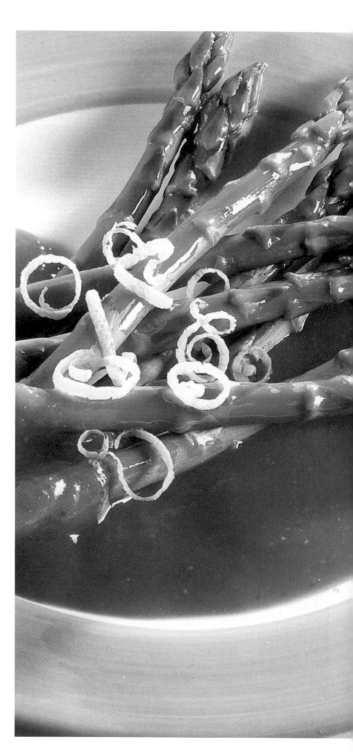

LEBANESE COUSCOUS SOUP

SERVES **6**

Couscous, tiny grains made from semolina, is usually steamed over a stew or stock.
In this recipe, the couscous has been used to thicken a richly spiced onion soup.

4 large onions, finely sliced

3 cloves garlic, finely sliced

3 tbsp olive oil

1 red chilli, deseeded and chopped finely

1 tsp mild chilli powder

¹/₂ tsp ground turmeric

1 tsp ground coriander

salt substitute (see page 18) and freshly ground
    black pepper

2.3 litres well-flavoured vegetable (see page 23) or
    chicken stock (see page 24)

50 g couscous

freshly chopped coriander to garnish

1 Cook the onions and garlic in the oil until well browned. This will take about 15 minutes over a medium high heat. You must let the onions brown to achieve a rich colour for the finished soup.

2 Stir in the chopped chilli and the spices and cook over a low heat for a further 1–2 minutes before adding the stock. Season lightly then bring to the boil. Cover and simmer for 30 minutes.

3 Stir the couscous into the soup, return to the boil, and simmer for a further 10 minutes. Season to taste then garnish with coriander and serve immediately.

NUTRITIONAL VALUES

VEGETABLE SNOW PANCAKES

SERVES **4**

Light pancakes made from egg whites and flavoured with spring onions are the ideal base on which to serve mixed vegetables. Large white radish peps up the already delicious broccoli and mushroom mixture.

2 egg whites

2 tbsp cornflour

salt substitute (see page 18)

2 spring onions, finely chopped

FOR THE STIR-FRIED VEGETABLES

225 g broccoli

225 g mushrooms, thinly sliced

3 tbsp gluten-free soy sauce

1 tbsp caster sugar

1 tbsp rice vinegar or cider vinegar

olive oil for cooking

3 tbsp sesame seeds

NUTRITIONAL VALUES

1   Lightly whisk the egg whites with 3 tablespoons water, adding the cornflour a teaspoonful at a time. Whisk in a little salt substitute, then stir in the spring onions.

2   Cut the white radish lengthways into thin slices, then cut the slices into fine strips. Place these in a bowl and set aside.

3   Cut the broccoli into small pieces and mix them with the radish. Place the mushroom slices in a separate bowl and add the soy sauce, sugar and vinegar. Mix well but try not to break up the mushroom slices. Cover and set the mixture aside.

4   The pancakes may be cooked individually in a wok or three to four at a time in a large frying pan. Heat a little oil, then lightly whisk the batter and pour a spoonful into the pan to make a thin round pancake. Cook until set and browned underneath, then turn and cook the second side until lightly browned. Drain the pancakes on absorbent kitchen paper and keep them hot. Make eight small pancakes.

5   Heat a little oil, then use a draining spoon to add the mushrooms. Stir-fry over high heat for about 1 minute, until the mushrooms are browned. Add the radish and broccoli and continue cooking for about 3 minutes. Stir in the sesame seeds and cook for 1 minute, then pour in the juices from marinating the mushrooms.

6   Arrange the pancakes on individual plates, then top each with a portion of the stir-fried vegetables. Serve at once.

SUMMER AVOCADO

SERVES **4**

This is a very refreshing starter with lots of citrus flavours.

2 ripe avocados

1 tbsp lemon juice

2 grapefruit

1 small lettuce

¼ cucumber

150 ml vinaigrette dressing

100 g cooked prawns

50 g yellow long-grain rice, cooked

1 yellow pepper, deseeded

freshly ground black pepper

1 Peel the avocados. Cut them in half and remove the stones. Cut the flesh in slices and pour on the lemon juice to prevent discolouration.

2 Using a small sharp knife, cut a slice from the grapefruit exposing the flesh. Cut round in strips removing all the white pith.

3 When the grapefruit are peeled and showing no pith, cut into each section between the membranes of each slice. At the end you will have segments of grapefruit without skin. Squeeze the juice of the membranes by hand over the fruit.

4 Line individual dishes with washed, drained lettuce leaves, and cucumber slices.

5 Pour some of the vinaigrette dressing over the grapefruit.

6 Mix the cooked prawns with the rice and dressing.

7 Cut the yellow pepper in thin strips. Retaining some for garnishing, chop the remainder and mix with the rice and prawns. Season well.

8 Arrange the prawn and rice mixture in the dishes on the cucumber and lettuce.

9 Top with sliced avocado and grapefruit. Garnish with pepper rings.

NUTRITIONAL VALUES

ORZO WITH PANCETTA AND PINE NUTS

SERVES **4**

A very tasty rice starter, also good served as an accompaniment to a main course.

120 g pancetta (other unsmoked bacon
   may be substituted)

2 tbsp olive oil

90 g pine nuts

150 g orzo

500 ml chicken stock (see page 24)

1½ tsp chopped fresh oregano leaves
   (or ½ tsp dried)

freshly ground black pepper to taste

NUTRITIONAL VALUES

1   Chop the pancetta and sauté it in the olive oil in a medium-size saucepan over medium heat until lightly browned. Remove with a slotted spoon to kitchen paper to drain.

2   Add the pine nuts to the saucepan and sauté, stirring constantly until browned, about 1–2 minutes. Remove with a slotted spoon to kitchen paper to drain. Add the orzo to the pan and sauté for about 1 minute, stirring constantly.

3   Add the stock, oregano, pepper, then bring the mixture to the boil. Lower the heat, cover the saucepan and simmer for 12–14 minutes, until all the stock is absorbed. Remove the saucepan from the heat.

4   Return the pancetta and pine nuts to the saucepan. Toss and serve.

SCALLOPS IN CHAMPAGNE SAUCE

SERVES **4**

This may sound rather extravagant, but it requires very little champagne.

8 large scallops (on the shell, if possible)

4 spring onions

chopped root ginger to taste

2 cloves of garlic

4 tbsp olive oil, warmed

1 glass champagne

chopped flat-leaf parsley

NUTRITIONAL VALUES

1 Remove the scallops from the shell, using a short bladed knife. Discard the black bits and keep the white flesh and the coral. Keep any liquor from the shell and reserve the shells.

2 Slice the spring onions, ginger, and garlic. Fry for a few minutes in the warmed oil, then add the sliced scallops and their liquor. Toss the shellfish and onion mixture over a high heat for about 5 minutes. Remove the large pieces from the pan with a slotted spoon and keep warm.

3 Pour the glass of champagne into the juices in the pan. Cook on a high heat until the sauce is reduced. Serve the chopped scallops on the deep half shell with the sauce. Garnish with the chopped parsley.

TAMARILLO AND AVOCADO COCKTAIL

SERVES **4**

This is an excellent appetizer, with an interesting blend of flavours. The egg-shaped tamarillo fruit is native to South America and is also known as a 'tree tomato'. It has a tough, bitter skin that needs to be peeled, and reveals tart golden pink flesh that is purple-tinged around the seeds.

3 tamarillos

shredded lettuce

75 g low-fat soft cheese with herbs and garlic

6 tbsp low-fat Greek yoghurt or low-fat sour cream

1 tsp caster sugar

3 spring onions or green onions, chopped

2 large ripe avocados

NUTRITIONAL VALUES

1 Peel the tamarillos thinly, halve them lengthways, and slice across. Arrange a little shredded lettuce on 4 individual plates.

2 Mix the cheese with the low-fat yoghurt or low-fat sour cream in a bowl. Sprinkle the superfine sugar over the tamarillos, mix in the chopped spring onion, and leave to stand for 15 minutes.

3 Quarter and peel the avocados and slice them across.

4 Arrange the avocado slices on the lettuce, top with the tamarillo mixture, and spoon the cheese and yoghurt dressing over the top.

MAIN COURSES

MIXED VEGETABLE TAGINE

SERVES **4**

This dish can be made with raisins – you may like to add them when you make it – it's a matter of taste. Serve the tagine over couscous or rice.

100 g chickpeas, soaked overnight, then drained
   and chopped

3 tbsp olive oil

4 small carrots, sliced

2 chopped onions

3 garlic cloves, chopped

1 green pepper, sliced thin

2 sliced courgette

1 tsp ground coriander

1 tsp ground cumin

3 tomatoes, chopped

575 ml vegetable stock (see page 23)

freshly ground black pepper

juice of 1 lemon

2 tbsp fresh chopped parsley, to garnish

4 spring onions, white part only, finely chopped,
   to garnish

1   Cook the chickpeas in plenty of boiling water until just tender; the time will mainly depend on the age and variety of the chickpeas.

2   Meanwhile, heat the oil in a pan, add the carrots and fry until browned. Remove and reserve. Add the onion and garlic to the pan and cook gently until soft and golden. Add the pepper and courgette and cook until softened. Stir in the spices and cook until fragrant, then add the tomatoes, carrots, stock and seasoning. Bring to the boil.

3   Drain the chickpeas, add to the vegetable mixture, cover and simmer for about 30 minutes until all the vegetables are tender. Stir in the lemon juice, and sprinkle over the parsley and spring onions.

NUTRITIONAL VALUES

PAELLA VEGETARIANA

SERVES **6**

This paella is so moist, full of flavour, and substantial, that you will scarcely notice it is meat-free. The green, red and yellow peppers add a vibrant splash of colour to the pale rice, while the tangy artichoke hearts, delicate peas, and juicy tomatoes ensure that this vegetarian meal will satisfy even the most avid carnivores.

60 ml olive oil

1 large yellow onion, chopped

5 cloves garlic, crushed

950 ml vegetable stock (see page 23)

450 g rice

1 small red pepper, cut into strips

1 small yellow pepper, cut into strips

4 medium tomatoes, deseeded and chopped

115 g frozen peas, defrosted

400 g artichoke hearts, tough outer leaves
   removed, and quartered

1 lemon

1 Heat the oil in a paella pan and sauté the onion and garlic until the onion is tender and translucent. At the same time, heat the stock in a separate saucepan until simmering.

2 Pour the rice into the paella pan and sauté for about 3 minutes. Add the peppers and tomatoes and cook for a further 3 minutes. Add the simmering vegetable stock and cook over medium heat for 20 minutes or until almost tender and almost all the liquid has been absorbed. Stir in the peas.

3 Sprinkle the artichoke hearts with a few drops of lemon juice and arrange over the rice in an attractive pattern. Continue cooking until the liquid has been absorbed and the rice is tender. Garnish with lemon wedges and serve.

NUTRITIONAL VALUES

PRAWN CREOLE

SERVES **4 – 6**

A great seafood dish, ideally served on a bed of white rice and garnished with coriander or parsley.

2 tbsp olive oil

1 large onion, chopped

8 cloves garlic, minced

2 large celery sticks, finely chopped

4 tomatoes, chopped

2 green peppers, cored, deseeded and chopped

2 tbsp tomato purée

1 tsp hot pepper sauce

1/2 tsp dried oregano

1 tsp dried thyme

2 tsp Worcestershire sauce

1.2 litres chicken stock (see page 24)

750 g prawns, shelled, and deveined

250 g can sliced water chestnuts, drained and rinsed, or 250 g jicama, sliced

1/2 tbsp lime juice

freshly ground black pepper

600 g cooked white long-grain rice

1 tbsp minced coriander or parsley to garnish

1   Heat the oil in a large saucepan, frying pan, or wok. Add the onion, garlic, celery, tomatoes and peppers and fry over medium heat until tender.

2   Add the tomato paste, hot pepper sauce, oregano and thyme and blend, stirring constantly, for about 2 minutes. Add the Worcestershire sauce and chicken stock and bring to the boil over medium-high heat for about 30 minutes until thickened.

3   Add the prawns and water chestnuts and simmer for about 4 minutes, uncovered, until the prawns are opaque.

4   Remove the pan from the heat and adjust the seasoning with more hot pepper sauce to taste, lime juice and pepper.

5   Serve over or under a scoop of rice on warm dishes and sprinkle the top with coriander or parsley.

6   Serve immediately.

NUTRITIONAL VALUES

FISH WITH BLACK BEANS

SERVES **4**

Serve this delicious fish dish with plain cooked rice. If it is included along with several other dishes as part of an extensive menu, the quantity of fish may be reduced by half.

900 g plaice or whiting, skinned

3 tbsp salted black beans

5 tbsp dry sherry

3 tbsp light gluten-free soy sauce

1 tsp sesame oil

25 g cornflour

3 tbsp olive oil

5 cm piece fresh ginger, peeled and cut in fine strips

1 green chilli, deseeded and cut into rings

1 clove garlic, crushed

1 piece lemon grass or strip of lemon rind

1 bunch spring onions, cut diagonally into strips

NUTRITIONAL VALUES

1 Cut the fish across into 1 cm wide strips and place these in a large shallow dish. Sprinkle the salted black beans, sherry, soy sauce, and sesame oil over the fish. Cover the dish and leave the strips to marinate for 2–3 hours.

2 When you are ready to cook the fish, drain the strips well, reserving all the juices. Toss the strips in the cornflour.

3 Heat the oil, then stir fry the ginger, chilli, garlic and lemon grass or rind over medium heat for 4–5 minutes, to extract their flavour. Add the fish strips to the pan and stir fry them carefully, avoiding breaking the strips, until they are lightly browned.

4 Add all the spring onions and continue to stir fry for 2 minutes, until the onions are cooked. Add 5 tablespoons water to the reserved marinating juices and pour them into the pan. Bring to the boil, reduce the heat and stir fry for 1 minute. Serve at once.

PRAWNS AND SCALLOPS WITH MUSHROOMS IN SPICY THAI SAUCE

SERVES **4**

Serve in a soup bowl with a spoonful of rice or a tangle of rice noodles alongside, to soak up the rich, spicy sauce.

10 dried mixed mushrooms such as shiitake, or Chinese black mushrooms

10 each dried small and large black fungus (tree cloud)

450 ml stock

5 shallots, chopped

5 garlic cloves, chopped

3 tbsp olive oil

½ tsp each turmeric and gluten-free curry powder

1 tsp ground coriander

1 tbsp chopped fresh root ginger

1 medium-hot fresh red chilli such as jalapeño, thinly sliced

1 carrot, sliced diagonally

¼ aubergine, cut into small bite-size pieces or diced

¼ red pepper, chopped

100–150 g common cultivated mushrooms, cut into bite-size pieces

3–4 kaffir lime leaves, fresh or dried

10–12 spears very thin asparagus, cut into bite-size lengths

90 g creamed coconut, in small pieces

8 each large prawns and scallops, trimmed and halved or quartered

juice of ½ lime, or as desired

1 Place the shiitake or Chinese black mushrooms and two types of black fungus in a saucepan with the stock. Bring to the boil, reduce the heat and simmer for about 5 minutes. Cover and leave while you prepare the rest of the dish.

2 Lightly sauté the shallots and garlic in the olive oil until softened, then sprinkle in the turmeric, curry powder, coriander, ginger, chilli, carrot, aubergine, red pepper and the rest of the mushrooms, and cook until the vegetables are half tender, about 5 minutes.

3 Remove the rehydrated mushrooms and fungus from the stock. Cut the large black fungus into smaller pieces, leaving the smaller fungus and the mushrooms whole. Strain the mushroom liquid.

4 Pour the strained liquid into the sautéeing vegetables, along with the lime leaves, and cook a few minutes together. Add the rehydrated mushrooms and fungus, the asparagus, prawns and scallops. Stir well but gently and add the creamed coconut, tossing gently over medium heat until the coconut has emulsified into the sauce. The asparagus and seafood should be just cooked through. Serve immediately, with a squeeze of lime.

NUTRITIONAL VALUES

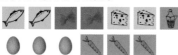

MOROCCAN FISH AND PEPPER BROCHETTES

SERVES **4**

The combination of fish with peppers and spices gives a real taste of north Africa.

5 garlic cloves, chopped

1/2 tsp each: paprika and cumin

several pinches cayenne pepper

1/2–1 tsp salt substitute (see page 18), or to taste

6 tbsp extra–virgin olive oil

2 tbsp each: fresh chopped parsley and coriander

juice of 1 lemon

500 g firm–fleshed white fish, cut into bite–sized
    pieces

1 each: red, yellow, green pepper, peeled, and cut
    into bite–sized pieces

1 lemon, cut into wedges

1 Combine the garlic, paprika, cumin, cayenne pepper, olive oil, 1 tablespoon of each of the parsley and coriander, and the lemon juice. Add the fish pieces and mix carefully, until thoroughly coated. Allow to marinate for 2 hours at room temperature or overnight in the refrigerator.

2 Thread onto skewers alternating with chunks of pepper.

3 Light the barbecue. Grill the brochettes over charcoal until slightly browned on each side, 7–8 minutes in total.

4 Serve sprinkled with the remaining parsley, coriander, and lemon wedges. Have hot sauce on the side, for those who enjoy a spicier flavour.

NUTRITIONAL VALUES

FRESH TUNA BRAISED BORDELAIS STYLE

SERVES **4**

This warming tuna dish is ideal to serve with wild rice and green beans.

6 tbsp olive oil

300 g fresh tuna

1 large onion

5 medium tomatoes

160 ml white wine

160 ml fish stock

450 g mushrooms

freshly ground black
pepper

1 Heat 4 tablespoons oil over a medium heat. Brown the fish in the oil on both sides – about 2 minutes per side. Thinly slice the onion and add to the fish.

2 As the onion is cooking, deseed and then dice the tomatoes. Add them to the mixture, together with the white wine and the fish stock. Bring the liquid to the boil, then lower the heat to a gentle simmer.

3 Cook the fish for 15 minutes, retrieve from the pan juices and set aside to keep warm.

4 With the remaining 1 tablespoon oil, fry the mushrooms until golden and add them to the pan juices. Turn up the heat and reduce by one-third. When the liquor is reduced, check the seasoning, pour over the tuna and serve immediately.

NUTRITIONAL VALUES

CURRIED RICE PILAF

SERVES **6 – 8**

A squeeze of lemon would bring out the flavour of this tasty rice dish, and is great served with chicken or shrimp kebabs.

4 tbsp olive oil

3 cloves garlic, crushed

300 g converted (par-boiled) rice

2 gluten-free chicken stock cubes

1 small red onion, diced

1 stick celery, diced

½ pimento, diced

1 tbsp gluten-free curry powder

1 tsp freshly ground black pepper

700 ml water

6 spring onions, thinly sliced

1 Heat the olive oil over a medium heat and sauté the garlic, stirring constantly. Add the rice and crumble in the chicken stock cubes. Sauté until golden brown, stirring frequently so the rice does not scorch.

2 Add the onions, celery, pimento, curry powder and pepper and cook, stirring, for 2 minutes.

3 Pour in the water and bring to the boil. Add the spring onions, cover and simmer for 5 minutes.

4 Remove from the heat and leave to stand for 30 minutes. Serve warm.

NUTRITIONAL VALUES

GRILLED HALIBUT STEAK WITH CARIBBEAN MARINADE

SERVES **4**

Halibut steaks are a great alternative to salmon steaks, especially if you want a less oily fish. They are thick enough to stand up to grilling without the aid of a grilling basket, which can't be said for a lot of other white-fleshed fish.

2 tbsp red wine vinegar

1 large onion, shredded

2 tbsp tomato purée

4 cloves garlic, crushed

2 tsp packed brown sugar

1 to 2 tbsp red chilli paste (optional)

2 tsp anchovy paste

4 halibut steaks (250 g each)

1 Combine all the ingredients except the halibut in a small bowl for the marinade, and mix well.

2 Place the fish in a glass baking dish. Pour the marinade over the fish, turning to coat all sides. Cover and marinate for 1 hour.

3 Remove the halibut from the dish, reserving some of the marinade. Grill over hot heat for about 6 minutes per side, brushing with the marinade while cooking.

NUTRITIONAL VALUES

ASIAN PRAWNS WITH HONEY-TEA DIPPING SAUCE

SERVES **4 – 6**

You can serve this Asian delight on a bed of citrus rice fried in a little ginger and garlic. To make extra-strong tea, simply use two tea bags with the usual amount of boiling water for one cup.

250 g of extra-strong orange spiced tea, cooled

125 ml honey

125 ml sweet rice vinegar

1 tbsp fresh lemon juice

1 tbsp grated root ginger

1 clove garlic, crushed

1 tsp ground coriander

1/2 tsp ground black pepper

700 g medium shrimp, peeled and deveined, with
   tails left on

salt substitute (see page 18), to taste

4 spring onions, thinly sliced (white and green parts)

orange wedges

8 metal skewers

NUTRITIONAL VALUES

1 Combine the tea, honey, vinegar, lemon juice, ginger, garlic, coriander and pepper and blend well. Reserve 125 ml of the marinade, cover, and set aside.

2 Place the prawns and the marinade in a rescalable plastic bag, seal and turn to coat. Marinate in the refrigerator for at least 30–45 minutes.

3 Remove the prawns from the bag, discarding the marinade. Thread them onto eight skewers, dividing them evenly, and alternating with orange wedges. Grill over medium heat, turning only once, for 4–6 minutes or until the prawns are just pink and firm to the touch. Be careful not to overcook. Season with salt substitute to taste.

4 To prepare the dipping sauce, add the reserved marinade to a pan. Bring to the boil over medium heat and reduce the sauce slightly, about 3–5 minutes. Stir in the spring onion. Serve hot.

ORANGE-GINGER MARINATED WHITEFISH

SERVES **4**

Marinating the fish in orange, ginger and onion gives it a delicious flavour and keeps it lovely and moist. A colourful and flavourful feast, it may be made with any white fish. A small grapefruit may be used in place of the orange, using only the flesh and not the zest.

4 large whitefish fillets, skinned
   (about 175 g each)
juice and zest of 1/2 medium orange
1 cm piece fresh ginger, shredded
2 cloves garlic, crushed
4 spring onions, shredded
1 medium orange, segmented
4 tbsp dry white wine
1–2 tbsp olive oil
1 tbsp fresh chives, chopped

NUTRITIONAL VALUES

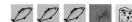

1   Rinse the fish under running water and pat dry. Place in a shallow glass dish. Mix half of the orange juice and zest, the ginger, garlic, spring onions and half of the orange segments in the dish. Cover and marinate for 1 hour, turning occasionally.

2   Remove the fish, orange and spring onions from the dish, reserving the marinade, and place in a greaseproof paper-lined steamer tier. Cover with a tight-fitting lid and steam for 10–15 minutes.

3   Meanwhile, pour the marinade into a small saucepan with the remaining orange juice, zest and the wine. Bring to the boil and boil rapidly for 2–3 minutes to reduce. Remove from the heat. Stir in the oil to give a glossy sauce and add the chives.

4   Serve the fish on warm plates with the sauce. Garnish with fresh chives and orange segments and serve with freshly steamed rice.

BRAISED QUAILS

SERVES 6

Served on a bed of freshly cooked pasta, this dish can be complemented with a crisp green salad or a selection of colourful vegetables such as carrots, fine green beans and parsnips.

4 tbsp olive oil

100 g onions

100 g celery

100 g carrots

6 quails

150 ml light stock

freshly ground black
    pepper to taste

1   Heat the oil over a medium heat.

2   Julienne – or very finely slice – the onions, celery and carrots. Lower the heat and simmer the vegetables in the oil for 5 minutes.

3   Add the quails, turn up the heat to seal the meat, then turn back to a simmer.

4   Add the stock, cover and cook slowly for 10 minutes, then season to taste and serve.

NUTRITIONAL VALUES

SKEWERED CHICKEN

SERVES **4**

A healthy and nutritious way of serving chicken to children. Delicious hot with rice or jacket potatoes, or cold as part of a packed lunch.

3 boneless chicken breasts (approx. 175 g each)

2 tbsp smooth peanut butter

2 tbsp low-fat natural yoghurt

freshly ground black pepper

shredded rind ½ orange

juice of 1 orange

1 tbsp clear honey

GARNISH

peeled orange segments

sprigs of watercress

NUTRITIONAL VALUES

1 Skin and cut the chicken breasts into small, even-sized cubes (approx. 2 cm). Thread them onto 8 small wooden kebab skewers, which have been soaked for ½ hour to stop them burning.

2 Mix together the peanut butter, yoghurt, orange rind and black pepper to taste. Spoon the mixture evenly over the skewered chicken. Cover loosely and chill for 4 hours.

3 Arrange the skewers on the rack of the grill pan, and spoon over any remaining marinade. Grill for 4 minutes under a moderate heat. Turn the skewers and grill for a further 3 minutes.

4 Mix the orange juice with the honey and spoon over the kebabs. Return to the grill for a further 2 minutes.

5 Serve hot or cold, garnished with orange segments and watercress.

CHICKEN AND BUTTER BEAN BOURGUIGNONNE

SERVES **4**

Beef Bourguignonne, the traditional dish of Burgundy, is rich and heavy – delicious, but often not to the taste of the health-conscious diner. This recipe, which uses the classic ingredients for the Bourguignonne sauce, uses a mixture of chicken and beans for a lighter dish.

125 g butter beans, soaked overnight

2 tbsp olive oil

4 chicken thighs

1 large onion, finely chopped

2 rashers smoked back bacon, diced

125 ml brandy

2 cloves garlic, crushed

4 sprigs fresh thyme

2 bay leaves

1 bouquet garni

freshly ground black pepper

1 tbsp tomato purée

425 ml full-bodied red wine

110 g sliced button mushrooms

low-fat soured cream and freshly chopped chives
   to garnish

NUTRITIONAL VALUES

1 Preheat oven to 180°C/gas mark 4. Rinse the beans thoroughly then bring to the boil in a pan of fresh water. Simmer until required.

2 Heat the oil in a flameproof casserole, then add the chicken thighs and cook quickly until browned all over. Remove the chicken with a slotted spoon; add the onion and bacon and cook until softened but not browned. Return the chicken to the casserole and remove the pan from the heat. Warm the brandy gently until it ignites. Pour the brandy into the pan and leave until the flames subside, then return the pan to the heat and add the garlic, herbs and seasonings. Mix the tomato purée with the wine and pour into the pan, adding a little water, if necessary, to cover the chicken. Bring to the boil, then cover the pan and cook in the preheated oven for 1¹/₂ hours.

3 Stir the mushrooms into the casserole; check the seasoning and that the beans are tender. Return the casserole to the oven for a further 15–20 minutes. Garnish with low-fat sour cream and chives.

CHICKEN AND SWEET POTATO CURRY

SERVES **4**

Curries do not take very long to prepare because they are mainly stir fried. The ingredients for the sauce should be blended to a thick paste before cooking. The sweet potato in this recipe makes the chicken go further, and the curry should be served with boiled rice or chapatis.

2 chicken breast fillets, skinned and diced

3 tbsp olive oil

250 g diced sweet potato

425 g water

3 tbsp fresh coriander leaves, torn

SAUCE

1 large onion

3 cloves garlic

1 green chilli, seeded and chopped roughly

2 tbsp tomato purée

1 tbsp mild gluten-free curry powder

1 tbsp gluten-free lime pickle or gluten-free spiced
   fruit chutney

1 tsp Demerara sugar

2.5 cm piece fresh root ginger, peeled and
   chopped

NUTRITIONAL VALUES

1 Purée all the ingredients for the sauce together in a blender or food processor until a thick paste forms. Cook the chicken in the oil in a large pan until it starts to brown, then add the sweet potato and cook until lightly browned all over.

2 Spoon the curry paste into the pan and cook slowly for 2–3 minutes. Stir in the water. Simmer slowly for 20–25 minutes, until the chicken is tender. Add a little more water, if necessary, during cooking. Season to taste, then add the coriander and serve.

CHICKEN AND WILD RICE SALAD

SERVES **4**

It is preferable to use saffron strands rather than saffron powder. Either soak the strands in warm water for a few minutes, then use both the strands and soaking liquor, or sprinkle straight into the dish at the beginning of cooking.

175 g long-grain and brown rice, cooked

225 g cooked chicken, chopped

1 small onion, peeled

150 ml well-flavoured gluten-free mayonnaise

100 g mushrooms, washed

1 tbsp lemon juice

4 tbsp sweetcorn (corn kernels)

7 black olives

freshly ground black pepper

1 lettuce

2 heads chicory

1 Cook the rice as directed on the packet of mixed long grain and wild rice (450 ml water – 225 g rice.) Allow to cool.

2 Add the chopped chicken to the cooled rice.

3 Chop the onion finely and add to the mixture with the mayonnaise.

4 Slice the mushrooms thinly. Mix with the rice, remembering to retain a few for the top of the salad. Pour the lemon juice over the retained mushrooms.

5 Add the sweetcorn and 4 chopped olives to the mixture. Season to taste.

6 Arrange the lettuce and sliced chicory in the salad bowl. Turn the chicken and rice mixture into the bowl.

7 To serve, garnish with the mushroom slices and the 3 remaining black olives.

NUTRITIONAL VALUES

CHICKEN PAELLA WITH SUN-DRIED TOMATOES

SERVES **6**

This sophisticated paella is typical of parts of Spain, where the sun-dried tomatoes are added for extra flavour. Here, the dried tomatoes are enhanced by the dry sherry, and provide a flavourful contrast to the plump rice.

28 g sun-dried tomatoes (not packed in olive oil), chopped

175 ml dry sherry, for soaking

120 ml olive oil

70o g skinless, boneless chicken breasts, cut into chunks

70 g sliced mushrooms

½ medium onion, finely chopped

3 cloves garlic, finely chopped

3 tbsp dry sherry

300 g rice

770 ml chicken stock

¼ tsp saffron

1 tsp dried basil

NUTRITIONAL VALUES

1 Soak the chopped sun-dried tomatoes in 175 ml sherry for 30 minutes, then drain when ready to use.

2 Heat the olive oil in a paella pan over medium heat. Add the chicken and fry until browned on all sides.

3 Meanwhile, in a small saucepan over low heat, cook the mushrooms, onion, and garlic in 3 tablespoons sherry until the mushrooms are tender. Add this mixture to the paella pan and stir well. Mix in the sun-dried tomatoes and cook for 3 minutes. Pour in the rice and cook for a further 5 minutes, stirring frequently. Add the stock, saffron, and basil and cook for about 25 minutes, or until the rice and chicken are tender and the stock has been absorbed. Serve at once.

PAELLA WITH CHICKEN, COURGETTE AND ROSEMARY

SERVES **6**

This delicately flavoured rice dish features tender chicken breasts subtly seasoned with fresh rosemary. A touch of dry sherry lends this paella extra Andalusian flair.

175 ml olive oil

1.3 kg chicken breasts, boned and cut into pieces

1 large onion, chopped

5 cloves garlic, minced

1 large green pepper, chopped

90 ml dry sherry

340 g rice

700 ml chicken stock (see page 24)

$1/4$ tsp saffron

$1/4$ tsp turmeric

3 tbsp chopped fresh rosemary

3 large courgette, cut into 4 cm strips

pepper, to taste

NUTRITIONAL VALUES

1 Heat 50 ml of the oil in a paella pan. Add the chicken and cook until done and browned on all sides. Set aside.

2 Clean the pan and heat the remaining olive oil over medium heat. Add the onion, and cook for 5 minutes. Add the garlic and green pepper and cook for 3 minutes. Add the sherry and cook for a further 1 minute. Pour in the rice and sauté for 5 minutes. Mix in the stock, saffron, turmeric, browned chicken, and $1^1/_2$ tablespoons of the rosemary and cook for 15 minutes.

3 Sprinkle in the remaining rosemary and stir. Arrange the courgettes over the rice, cover, and cook for a further 10 minutes or until the rice and chicken are tender, and the stock has been absorbed. Allow to cool for 5 minutes, and serve.

PISTACHIO ROASTED CHICKEN

SERVES **6 – 8**

This is a variation of one of Greece's most popular dishes. The chicken should be cut up into pieces and served with the stuffing separately.

50 ml olive oil

2 onions, finely chopped

225 g long-grain rice

4 large tomatoes, skinned, deseeded and chopped

225 g shelled pistachio nuts, roughly chopped

pinch of ground cinnamon

freshly ground black pepper

525 ml boiling water

3 tbsp very finely chopped fresh parsley

45 ml prepared chicken, without giblets

50 ml dry white wine

1 Preheat the oven to 230°C/gas mark 8. Heat half of the olive oil in a large, heavy frying pan and sauté the onion for about 5 minutes or until softened.

2 Add the rice to the frying pan and continue to cook for a further 3 minutes or until the rice begins to brown, stirring occasionally. Add half of the tomatoes, the pistachios, cinnamon and freshly ground black pepper and 175 ml boiling water. Simmer for about 10 minutes or until the liquid is mostly absorbed and the rice is almost cooked, stirring continuously. Remove from the heat and stir in the parsley.

3 Spoon the rice mixture into the cavity of the chicken without packing it too firmly. Place the chicken in a roasting tin and spoon any remaining rice mixture around the outside. Season the chicken with freshly ground black pepper.

4 Scatter the remaining chopped tomatoes around the chicken and pour 350 ml boiling water and the wine into the tin. Reduce the oven temperature to 180°C/gas mark 4 (the chicken skin is seared and made crispy before the oven adjusts to the lower heat). Drizzle the remaining olive oil over the chicken and roast for about 1½ hours or until the chicken is cooked through and the rice, inside and outside of the chicken, is tender. Baste the chicken during cooking and add a little extra water if necessary. Let it stand for 10 minutes before serving it with the stuffing.

NUTRITIONAL VALUES

FRUIT CHICKEN KEBABS WITH CURRIED HONEY GLAZE

SERVES 4

Kebabs are perfect for both a summer barbecue or a winter supper. They can be made well in advance and the ingredients can be varied to suit your own preference.

4 large boneless chicken breasts, skinned

8 rashers streaky bacon, diced

16 dried apricot halves (non-soak variety)

2 firm bananas, cut into
    2.5 cm slices

1 tbsp lemon juice

MARINADE

90 ml clear honey

60 ml light olive oil

rind and juice 1 orange

2 cloves garlic, crushed

1 tbsp gluten-free Worcestershire sauce

1 tsp coriander seeds, crushed

1 tsp gluten-free curry powder

NUTRITIONAL VALUES

1. Shake all the marinade ingredients together in a screw top jar.

2. Cut the chicken into neat 2.5 cm cubes. Place in a bowl and pour over the marinade. Cover and keep in a refrigerator for 6 hours, or until required.

3. Stretch the bacon rashers with the back of a knife. Cut each into half and form into rolls.

4. Alternately thread pieces of chicken, apricot halves, banana chunks and bacon rolls onto skewers.

5. Brush with the remaining marinade and cook for 10–15 minutes under a pre-heated grill turning and basting frequently, until the chicken is cooked and sizzling.

6. Serve warm with crusty bread and salad.

FRIED NOODLES WITH CHICKEN, VEGETABLES AND GRAVY

SERVES **4**

If available, use the large flat noodles known as 'sen yai', *rather than the thin variety.*

300 g large flat rice noodles (sen yai)

100 ml peanut or corn oil

1 tsp gluten-free black soya sauce

2 tbsp garlic, chopped finely

200 g boneless skinned chicken breasts cut
   lengthways into 1 cm thick slices

2 tbsp gluten-free white soya sauce

2 tbsp sugar

1 tsp ground white pepper

1.35 litres chicken stock

400 g kale or broccoli, cut into 1 cm pieces

1 tbsp cornflour, mixed with a little water

NUTRITIONAL VALUES

1 Boil the noodles for 1 minute and drain well. Heat half the oil in a wok or pan, add the noodles and fry lightly for 1 minute. Add the black soya sauce, fry lightly for another minute. Drain off the oil and transfer the noodles to a plate.

2 Heat the rest of the oil in the wok. Add the garlic and chicken, and fry lightly for 2 minutes. Stir in the white soya sauce, sugar, white pepper and then the chicken stock. Boil well for 3–5 minutes, add the kale, boil again for 1 minute and then add the cornflour. Boil for 1 minute and pour over the noodles.

3 Serve accompanied by phrik dong (sliced fried red chilli in vinegar), fish sauce, sugar and chilli powder, in separate bowls.

CARIBBEAN CHICKEN AND RICE STEW

SERVES **6**

This tasty chicken stew comes from Puerto Rico.

1 garlic clove, chopped

1/2 tsp dried oregano (marjoram)

1.5 kg chicken, cut into 8 pieces

4 tbsp olive oil

1 small onion, finely chopped

150 g green peppers, chopped

4 ripe tomatoes, skinned and
 chopped

350 g uncooked long-grain
 white rice

2.25 litres chicken stock (see
 page 24)

freshly ground black pepper

450 g frozen peas

50 g Parmesan cheese, freshly
 grated

1 fresh hot pepper, chopped

NUTRITIONAL VALUES

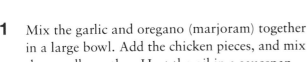

1 Mix the garlic and oregano (marjoram) together in a large bowl. Add the chicken pieces, and mix them well together. Heat the oil in a saucepan, and brown the chicken pieces. Transfer them to a plate.

2 Add the onion and green peppers to the pan, and cook until soft.

3 Add the tomatoes and browned chicken pieces, coating them well with the onion, peppers and tomato mixture. Reduce the heat and simmer for 30 minutes, or until the chicken is cooked.

4 Remove the chicken to a plate and leave to cool a little.

5 Remove the bones, and cut the flesh into 5 cm pieces.

6 Meanwhile, add the rice, stock and freshly ground black pepper to the onion, peppers, and tomato mixture, and bring to the boil. Reduce the heat, cover, and simmer for 20 minutes or until the rice is cooked.

7 Stir in the peas, Parmesan, and hot pepper. Mix well, then ad the chicken. Cover and simmer for 2 more minutes, then serve.

ROAST CHICKEN WITH MUSHROOM AND RICE TIMBALES

SERVES **4**

This tasty chicken dish is beatifully complemented by the mushroom and rice moulds, which looks particularly appetizing.

1.5 kg roasting chicken

½ lemon

1 bay leaf

¼ onion, peeled

sprig of thyme or 1 tsp mixed herbs

2 tbsp olive oil

RICE TIMBALES

100 g mushrooms, washed and sliced

50 g butter

2 tbsp lemon juice

225 g long-grain rice, cooked

freshly ground black pepper

1 tbsp parsley, chopped

1 tbsp grated cheese

1 small carrot (optional)

GRAVY

1 small onion

1 bay leaf

300 ml chicken stock (see page 24)

2 tbsp white wine (optional)

1 Rub over the chicken with the halved lemon. Place the lemon, bay leaf, onion, and herbs inside the cavity of the chicken with a drop of olive oil.

2 Rub the remaining olive oil over the chicken skin and place in a pre-heated oven at 200°C/gas mark 6. Cook for approximately 1 hour 20 minutes or until chicken is tender.

3 Slice the mushrooms. Heat the butter in a frying pan and sauté the mushrooms for 3 minutes. Add the lemon juice. Cover the pan and allow all moisture to evaporate without burning the mushrooms.

4 Have the rice already cooked by the absorption method. Mix with pepper, parsley, and grated cheese.

5 Oil small moulds or ramekin dishes well. Arrange mushroom slices on the bottom. If you wish, slice some carrot with a cocktail cutter for extra decoration. Blanch the slices in boiling water for 4 minutes, then add to the mushroom design. Mix remaining sliced mushrooms with the rice. Turn the rice into the moulds and pack down well.

6 Place the moulds in the oven for the last 20 minutes of the chicken's cooking time.

7 Remove the chicken and moulds from the oven and allow to stand for 10 minutes before carving and turning out the timbales.

8 To make gravy remove the chicken from the roasting pan and keep warm. Pour off excess fat. If giblets come with the chicken simmer these for at least 30 minutes with an onion, bay leaf, and water for stock. Otherwise use bought chicken stock. Add the stock to the chicken juice in the roasting pan which can be placed over a low heat. Add seasoning and, for extra special gravy, white wine. Reduce by simmering gently. Serve in a heated sauce boat.

9 Carve the chicken and serve 1–2 rice timbales with each portion.

NUTRITIONAL VALUES

CROWN ROAST OF LAMB WITH APRICOT RICE STUFFING

SERVES **4**

This is an excellent dinner party dish as it can be prepared in advance.

2 best ends of neck (lamb)

3 tbsp olive oil

freshly ground pepper

STUFFING

100 g long-grain or risotto rice

1 onion, peeled and finely chopped

2 sticks of celery

100 g dried apricots, steeped or 1 large can
   apricots

1 tbsp sultanas

1 tbsp chopped mixed nuts

1 egg, beaten

1 tbsp chopped parsley

freshly ground black pepper

Oven temperature 180°C/gas mark 4

NUTRITIONAL VALUES

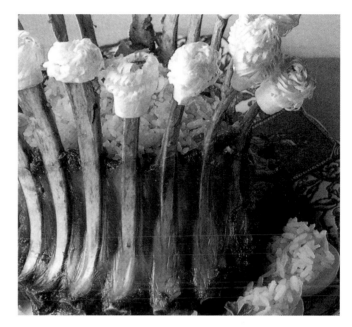

1   Ask the butcher to prepare the crown roast or, if this is not possible, have the best ends chined. Remove the skin from the fatty side of the joints. Cut along the fat about 3.5 cm from the top of the bone and remove fat and meat from the tops of the bones. Scrape the little end bones clean with a knife. Turn the meat over the cut between the cutlets to enable the roast (joint) to bend. Stand the two pieces of meat up with the bones at the top. Turn fatty sides in and sew together at the top and bottom of the joins to make the crown roast. Paint over with oil and sprinkle with pepper.

2   For the stuffing, partially cook the rice for 10 minutes, rinse, and allow to drain and cool.

3   Heat the oil and cook the onions for 4 minutes over a low heat. Add the chopped celery, chopped apricots (if using canned apricots retain 8 drained halves for garnish), sultanas and nuts. Lastly stir in the rice. Turn into a bowl and allow to cool. Mix with the egg yolk and parsley.

4   Fill the centre of the roast with the stuffing. Cover with a piece of foil.

5   Cover the individual tips of the bones with foil to prevent charring. Then completely cover with foil. Roast in the oven at 180°C/gas mark 4 for 1½–2 hours, depending on size of the cutlets.

6   Any excess stuffing may be used to stuff apricot halves which can be cooked brushed with oil for the last 30 minutes of cooking time.

7   Remove the crown roast to a heating plate and make gravy to accompany roast in the usual way. If using canned apricots, a little juice may be added to the gravy. Remove the string before carving through the cutlets.

BREDIE

Bredie is a South African stew of mutton, tomato juice and dried spotted beans similar to pinto beans. Its exotic combination of seasonings – cardamom, fennel and ginger – also includes some form of chillies.

2 lamb shanks

2 bay leaves

175 g dried pinto beans, picked and soaked
  overnight

2 tbsp olive oil

1 large onion, chopped

2 garlic cloves, minced

1 tsp fresh ginger, shredded

1 tsp ground coriander

1 tsp fennel seed

1/2 tsp dried thyme

1 tsp dried marjoram (oregano)

2 tbsp gluten-free chilli powder

450 ml tomato juice

175 g can tomato purée

Tabasco sauce to taste

1 Put the lamb shanks and bay leaves in a stockpot and cover with water. Bring to the boil, reduce heat, and simmer for 45 minutes. Drain the beans and add to the lamb. Add enough water to cover by 2.5 cm. Return to the boil, reduce heat and simmer for 30 minutes. Remove the lamb shanks and let cool slightly while you prepare the other ingredients.

2 Heat the oil in a large frying pan and sauté the onion and garlic for 2 minutes. Add the ginger, coriander, cardamom, fennel seed, thyme and marjoram (oregano), and sauté for 5 minutes longer. Add to the beans. Add the chilli powder, tomato juice and tomato purée to the beans. Return to the boil, reduce heat and continue simmering, stirring occasionally and adding water if needed.

3 When the lamb has cooled enough to handle, cut the meat and fat from the bones. Discard the fat and bones. Shred the meat and add it to the beans. When the beans are tender – about 1 1/2 hours total cooking time – add Tabasco to taste.

NUTRITIONAL VALUES

FESTIVAL PILAU WITH GROUND LAMB

SERVES **8**

Pilau is basically a rice dish in which the rice is first lightly fried, then steamed. A variety of delicious things may be added, like nuts and raisins. It is eaten in one form or another throughout Asia, from the Middle East to India.

2 limes or 1 pomegranate

300 g minced lamb

375 ml low-fat yoghurt

1 tsp ground anise

1 tbsp olive oil

4 cloves, braised

1 cinnamon stick

3 cardamom pods, bruised

2 bay leaves

100 g shelled pine nuts

75 g blanched almonds

450 g long-grain brown rice, soaked in water for 1
   hour and drained

75 g sultanas

300 g prunes, pitted and chopped

300 g dried apricots, chopped

4 large green apples

1 Squeeze the limes into a bowl, or put the pomegranate seeds into the bowl, being careful to discard all the connective tissue. Toss the lamb in the lime juice or seeds. Stir the yoghurt and anise into the lamb and leave it marinate while you prepare the rest of the dish.

2 Heat the oil in a large non-stick frying pan. Add the cloves, cinnamon, cardamom, bay leaves, pine nuts and almonds and stir-fry until the ingredients give off an aroma. Add the rice and continue stir-frying until the grains are transparent, about 8 minutes.

3 Transfer the mixture to a deep saucepan and add 1 litre boiling water. Put a double layer of cheesecloth over the top of the pan, then add the pan lid, making sure it is a tight fit. Steam the rice over very low heat for 15 minutes.

4 Once the rice is cooked, with wetted hands, roll the lamb into tiny thumbnail-sized balls. Sauté these lamb balls in the non-stick frying pan until they are no longer red on the outside.

5 Add the meatballs, sultanas, prunes and apricots to the rice mixture. Stir well, cover with another paper towel and the lid, and cook for another 15 minutes.

6 To serve, hollow out the centres of the apples, so that the fruit is cup-shaped. Place a candle in each apple, and arrange the apples around a serving platter. Pile the rice into the centre of the platter and light the candles just before serving.

NUTRITIONAL VALUES

LAMB IN MACADAMIA CREAM SAUCE

SERVES **6 – 8**

This is best served with rice and garnished with sliced macadamias and chopped coriander or parsley.

150 g macadamia nuts

2 medium-size onions, each cut into 16 pieces

30 g chopped fresh ginger

175 g plain yoghurt

2 tbsp coriander

1 tbsp ground cardamom

1 tsp freshly ground black pepper

salt substitute (see page 18)

90 g raisins

1.25 kg boneless leg of lamb, trimmed of all fat and cut into 3 cm cubes

chopped coriander or parsley leaves for garnish

1 With a sharp knife, thinly slice 30 g of the macadamia nuts. Don't worry if pieces crumble, ideally, however, they should resemble shaved chocolate. Refrigerate in an airtight container until needed.

2 Place the remaining 120 g of nuts in a blender or food processor fitted with a steel blade along with the onions, ginger and yoghurt. Process, stopping to scrape the bowl occasionally until the mixture resembles porridge.

3 Place the purée in a large, heavy saucepan or frying pan along with the coriander, cardamom, pepper, yoghurt, raisins and lamb. Bring to a simmer over medium heat. Lower the heat, cover, and simmer for 1 hour 30 minutes, stirring gently often during cooking to prevent sticking.

4 Uncover, add salt substitute to taste and raise the heat slightly. Continue to simmer for 30 to 45 minutes more, until the meat is very tender and the sauce has thickened. This dish is best made early in the day and allowed to mellow at room temperature, then reheated gently. Or it may be made a day in advance and refrigerated before reheating.

NUTRITIONAL VALUES

RICE WITH PORK AND PEPPERS

SERVES **4**

A very appetizing and easy to cook main course.

4 tbsp olive oil

1 large onion, thinly sliced

350 g lean boneless pork, cut in thin strips

1 red pepper, deseeded and thinly sliced

1 green pepper, deseeded and thinly sliced

freshly ground black pepper

a little grated nutmeg

grated rind of 1 orange

100 g long-grain rice, freshly cooked

100 g brown rice, freshly cooked

1 Heat the oil and stir-fry the onion for 2 minutes before adding the pork. Stir-fry the meat and onion together until the meat is cooked through and lightly browned, keeping the heat fairly high to seal the strips of meat.

2 Add the peppers, seasoning, nutmeg and orange rind. Reduce the heat slightly and stir-fry for 3–5 minutes, or until the peppers are cooked.

3 Stir in both types of rice and cook for a few minutes so that the ingredients are well combined. If the rice has been allowed to cool, it should be reheated thoroughly at this stage – the result is best if the rice is freshly cooked and piping hot when added to the pan.

NUTRITIONAL VALUES

STIR-FRIED PORK IN GINGER AND ONION

SERVES **4**

The sweet, tangy flavours of the soy sauce and ginger marinade are enriched and enhanced by the pork. Like most other Japanese dishes, this is easy to prepare and can be made in no time at all.

225 g sliced pork, cut into 5 cm lengths

4 tbsp olive oil

1 medium-sized onion, peeled and sliced

FOR THE MARINADE

25 g root ginger, peeled, grated and squeezed

1½ tbsp gluten-free soy sauce

1 tbsp sake

1   To make the marinade, mix together the juice of the ginger, the soy sauce, and the sake in a bowl.

2   Add the pork and marinate for 30 minutes. Heat the oil in a frying pan and fry the onion until it is transparent. Remove and set aside.

3   Add the meat to the frying pan and fry for 5 minutes or until cooked.

4   Return the onion to the frying pan and stir-fry for a further 1–2 minutes.

5   Add the remaining marinade and stir-fry again for 1–2 minutes. Serve with a bowl of hot, plain boiled rice.

NUTRITIONAL VALUES

SPICED MINCED BEEF AND LENTIL CUTLETS

SERVES **2-4**

A very colourful and tasty dish, served on a plate and decorated with sesame seeds.

4 small courgettes, cut diagonally into 5 mm slices

salt substitute (see page 18)

115 g lean beef, freshly ground

2 tbsp olive oil

2 spring onion, white and green parts very thinly sliced

1 tbsp sugar

1 tbsp gluten-free soy sauce

1/2–1 tsp gluten-free chilli powder

toasted sesame seeds for garnish

MARINADE

1 spring onion, white and green part very thinly sliced

2 garlic cloves, crushed and finely chopped

1 1/2 tbsp gluten-free soy sauce

1 tbsp sesame oil

2.5 cm piece of fresh ginger, finely chopped

1 tbsp toasted sesame seeds

freshly ground black pepper

NUTRITIONAL VALUES

1 Put the courgettes in a colander, sprinkle generously with salt substitute, toss together and leave for 30 minutes. Meanwhile mix all the marinade ingredients together, add the ground beef and leave for 30 minutes.

2 Rinse the courgettes well and dry thoroughly with paper towels. Heat the olive oil in a large frying pan over a fairly high heat, add the beef and marinade and fry, stirring to break up the lumps, for about 1 minute or until the beef changes colour.

3 Gently stir in the courgettes then add the remaining ingredients, except the sesame seeds. Cook for 2 minutes, stirring gently. Lower the heat and continue to stir for a further minute until the courgettes are tender but still retain some bite.

NASI GORENG

You can vary the amount of steak, prawn, omelette, and rice in this Indonesian dish. This gluten-free main course recipe is delicious and filling.

2 eggs

180 g raw prawns

350 g flank or rump steak

1 onion, chopped

2 garlic cloves, crushed

4 tbsp olive oil

4 spring onions, thinly sliced

350 g cooked rice

4 tsp gluten-free soy sauce

salt substitute (see page 18) and freshly ground
   black pepper

2 tbsp dried onion flakes, roasted

1/2 cucumber, sliced into strips

1 Make an omelette with the 2 eggs and slice into strips. Set aside. Shell and devein the prawns and boil the shells in water to make a fish stock. Shred the beef into thin strips.

2 In a blender blend together the onion, garlic and strained fish stock with 12 tablespoons of the oil. Pour this into a pan or wok and reduce to a purée. Add the rest of the oil, stir in the meat and prawns and cook until firm. Add the spring onion and rice, mix together, and sprinkle with soy sauce. Season to taste with salt substitute and pepper.

3 Turn onto a serving dish and garnish with the omelette strips, onion flakes and cucumber.

NUTRITIONAL VALUES

DESSERTS

ISRAELI ORANGE SORBET

Citrus fruits are a delicious and refreshing way to end a meal. Sorbets and ices are especially popular during the summer, but can be enjoyed all year round.

250 g sugar

grated zest and rind of 1 lemon

grated zest of 3 oranges

450 g fresh-squeezed orange juice, strained

2 egg whites, beaten to soft peaks

fresh mint leaves for garnish

sabria (or other orange-flavour liqueur) for serving

NUTRITIONAL VALUES

1 In a small heavy saucepan, combine sugar, lemon and orange zests and 250 ml water. Slowly bring to the boil, stirring until sugar dissolves. Cook 5 minutes, remove from heat and cool and refrigerate 3–4 hours or overnight.

2 Combine lemon and orange juices with the chilled syrup and, if you like, strain for a very smooth sorbet.

3 If using an ice-cream machine, freeze according to manufacturer's directions.

4 Alternatively, put into a metal bowl and freeze 3 to 4 hours until semi-frozen. Place into a food processor fitted with metal blade, scrape the semi-frozen mixture; process until light and creamy, 30–45 seconds. Return to metal bowl and freeze another 1½ hours. Scrape into food processor again and process with beaten egg whites until well mixed and light and creamy, 30 seconds. Freeze 3–4 hours until completely firm.

5 Soften 5 minutes at room temperature before scooping into individual serving glasses. Garnish with a few mint leaves and pass around the liqueur, allowing each guest to pour a little over the sorbet.

SPICED PEARS

SERVES **4**

The aroma from this dish is almost as good as the taste, and all part of the enjoyment. If you like, serve with a spoonful of plain low-fat yoghurt.

4 large ripe pears, peeled, halved and
  cored

375 ml mango juice

1 cinnamon stick, crushed

1/2 tsp grated nutmeg

3 tbsp raisins

2 tbsp granulated brown sugar

1 Place the pear halves in a pan with the fruit juice, spices, raisins and sugar. Heat gently to dissolve the sugar and then bring to the boil.

2 Reduce the heat to a simmer and cook for 10 minutes more until the pears are softened. Serve hot with the syrup.

NUTRITIONAL VALUES

GRAPE AND VERMOUTH GRANITA

SERVES **4**

A wonderfully cool and refreshing dessert to end any meal.

100 g granulated sugar

juice and grated rind 1 lemon

350 g white grapes

4 x 4 tbsp vermouth

TO DECORATE

4 small bunches of red grapes

4 x 4 tsp red grape juice, chilled

1 Place the sugar and 300 ml water in a saucepan, bring to the boil, stirring to dissolve the sugar.

2 Boil for 4 minutes, then stir in the lemon rind and juice.

3 Purée the grapes in a food processor or liquidizer, then pass through a sieve, to give a fine purée. Add to the syrup with the vermouth.

4 Cool, then transfer to a shallow freezer proof container. Freeze until slushy, then stir to scrape the ice crystals from the outside to the centre.

5 Freeze until firm, then break up into tiny pieces using a fork.

6 To serve, chill four glasses, spoon the grape and vermouth crystals into each and decorate with a bunch of grapes. Pour a teaspoon of red grape juice over each one and serve immediately.

NUTRITIONAL VALUES

POACHED PEARS WITH MANGO SAUCE

SERVES **4**

These are served immediately, carefully arranged on plates with green leaves with a little mango purée poured over the top.

4 medium sized pears

1 x 1 tbsp lemon juice

100 g sugar

1 cinnamon stick

strip of lemon zest

4 cloves

150 ml dry white wine

TO SERVE

green leaves (optional)

1 small mango, stoned and puréed

NUTRITIONAL VALUES

1 Peel the pears, but leave the stalks attached. Place in a bowl of water with the lemon juice to prevent them turning brown.

2 Place 300 ml water in a pan large enough to contain the pears upright side by side. Add the sugar, cinnamon and lemon zest. Bring to the boil, stirring to dissolve the sugar.

3 Stud the bases of each pear with a clove, add to the syrup with the wine. Cover and cook for 20–22 minutes, until tender.

4 Transfer the pears to a serving dish, boil the syrup to reduce by half, pour over the pears and leave to cool and chill.

5 To serve the pears, arrange on serving plates with green leaves if wished. Pour over a little mango purée and serve immediately.

CITRUS FLAMBE

SERVES **6**

This is a great citrus dessert and looks impressive, especially if you have guests when lighting the brandy.

2 pink grapefruit, peeled, pith removed

1 ugli, peeled, pith removed

6 tbsp brandy

50 g butter

50 g caster sugar

$1/2$ tsp ground cinnamon

$1/2$ tsp shredded nutmeg

4 oranges or tangerines, peeled, pith removed and
   sliced

NUTRITIONAL VALUES

1 Remove the segments of fruit from the grapefruit and ugli over a bowl to catch the juices.

2 Pour the brandy into a small bowl and place in a larger bowl of hot water to warm.

3 Place the butter, sugar and spices in a heavy based or flambé dish. Heat gently to dissolve. Add the fruit juice and heat until the sauce is syrupy.

4 Add the orange slices, grapefruit and ugli segments and cook gently to heat through.

5 Turn off the heat, pour the brandy over and carefully set alight with a taper. Let the flames die completely before serving.

ORANGE FLAN

SERVES 4

While most flans resemble traditional custard desserts, this flan from Spain is infused with a delicate orange flavour, a lingering reminder of the country's Moorish past.

150 g sugar, for the caramel topping

125 ml water, for the caramel topping

450 ml freshly squeezed orange juice

grated rind of 1 orange

4 medium eggs

2 medium egg yolks

150 g sugar

orange slices, to decorate

NUTRITIONAL VALUES

1. Preheat the oven to 180°C/gas mark 4. To make the caramel topping, heat the sugar and the water in a small saucepan, swirling gently until a golden brown caramel is formed. Immediately divide the mixture evenly among four individual ramekins. Swirl and tilt the ramekins to ensure that the caramel coats the ramekins' sides and bases. Place the ramekins in a baking pan.

2. In a small bowl, bring the orange juice and orange rind to the boil, then remove from the heat. Meanwhile, in a separate bowl, whisk together the eggs and egg yolks with the remaining sugar, until the mixture is thick. Pour in the orange juice and rind, stirring constantly.

3. Divide the mixture among the four ramekins in the baking pan, then pour boiling water around them to create a bain-marie. Bake in the oven for about 25 minutes or until lightly set. Allow to cool, then refrigerate overnight.

4. Immediately before serving, briefly immerse the bases of the ramekins in hot water and, if necessary, pass a knife around the outer edges of the ramekins to make unmoulding easier. Inverse and unmould the desserts on to serving saucers. Decorate with fresh orange slices.

TIPSY GREENGAGE SYLLABUB

SERVES **3 – 4**

You may not have come across this dessert before, but once you have given it a try it is sure to become a firm favourite.

2 tbsp granulated (castor) sugar

450 g greengages, halved and stoned

300 ml low-fat double cream

2 tbsp brandy

1 egg white

TO SERVE

pistachio nuts, chopped

lemon geranium leaves

NUTRITIONAL VALUES

1 Place the sugar and 150 ml water in a heavy based saucepan. Bring to the boil, stirring to dissolve the sugar. Boil for two minutes.

2 Add the greengages and simmer for 3–8 minutes, until tender but still holding their shape.

3 Divide the greengages and syrup in half and leave to cool. Purée one half.

4 Drain the remaining greengages and place at the bottom of a serving dish.

5 Whip the low-fat cream until it holds its shape, then whisk in the brandy, and fold in the purée.

6 Whisk the egg white and fold into the low-fat cream. Pour over the greengages, pistachio nuts, and lemon geranium leaves and serve.

ICED BLACKCURRANT SOUFFLÉ

MAKES **6**

This beautiful, richly-coloured soufflé makes great use of the sharp, refreshing taste of blackcurrants.

450 g blackcurrants, hulled

150 g sugar

2 egg whites

100 g icing sugar, sifted

300 ml low-fat whipping cream

NUTRITIONAL VALUES

1 Wrap a double thickness of aluminium foil around a 600 ml soufflé dish to extend 5 cm above the rim of the dish. Cook the blackcurrants with the sugar until soft, purée in a blender, and then strain. Allow to cool. Whisk the egg whites until stiff, then gradually whisk in the icing sugar.

2 Whip the low-fat cream until softly stiff. Place the fruit purée in a large bowl and gradually fold in the egg white and low-fat cream. Pour into the prepared soufflé dish, level the surface, and freeze for several hours until solid. Remove the foil and serve.

GRAPE CUSTARDS

SERVES **4**

This delightful dessert is so quick and simple to make. It is ideal for a dinner party.

225 g seedless red grapes

4 egg yolks

3 tbsp superfine sugar

4 tbsp marsala, madeira, or sweet sherry

NUTRITIONAL VALUES

1 Wash the grapes and place in the bottom of four individual glasses. Place the egg yolks in a bowl. Beat lightly, add the sugar and wine and mix together. Place the bowl over a pan of hot water and whisk until the mixture is thick and creamy. This could take about 10 minutes.

2 Divide the mixture among the glasses and serve at once while still warm with lady fingers.

FRUIT SALAD

SERVES **4**

A lovely fruity and juicy dessert, and very easy to make.

2 medium-sized juicy oranges

2 limes

30 g raspberries

30 g golden raspberries

30 g strawberries

30 g blueberries

30 g blackberries

1 large papaya

2 kiwi fruit, peeled and sliced

20 g fresh coconut meat, grated, or 25 g
   dessicated coconut

1 With a sharp paring knife, remove all skin from the oranges. Holding the oranges over a medium bowl to catch juices, cut along the membranes of the oranges so the segments fall into the bowl as well. Repeat the process for the limes.

2 Add raspberries, strawberries, blueberries and blackberries. Cover and refrigerate for 2 hours.

3 Peel papaya, cut in half and remove the seeds. Cut each half in 1 cm slices and arrange on 4 plates with sliced kiwi fruit.

4 Spoon berry and orange mixture, with juices, over papaya. Sprinkle with coconut.

NUTRITIONAL VALUES

DRIED FRUIT COMPOTE

SERVES **10-12**

Any combination of fruits can be used and the poaching liquid can range from water to tea, fruit juice or wine. You can experiment with this. Serve with a dollop of low-fat yoghurt or low-fat sour cream to cut the natural sweetness.

215 g large pitted prunes

215 g dried no-soak apricots

215 g dried no-soak pears

100 g dried no-soak peaches

100 g dried no-soak apple rings

90 g raisins

4 tbsp honey or sugar (optional)

grated zest and juice of 1 lemon

grated zest and juice of 1 orange

4–6 whole cloves

1 cinnamon stick

1 tbsp black peppercorns (optional)

slivered blanched almonds, toasted, for garnish

1 Into a large non-aluminium saucepan, place prunes, apricots, pears, peaches, apple rings and raisins. Cover with 2 litres water or enough to generously cover fruit.

2 Stir in honey or sugar to taste, if using, and add grated lemon and orange zests and juices, cloves, cinnamon stick and peppercorns, if using. Over high heat, bring to the boil. Cook, covered, over low heat, until fruit is plump and tender, 20 minutes.

3 With slotted spoon, remove cloves, cinnamon stick and peppercorns. Spoon fruit into a serving bowl and pour liquid over. Chill 3–4 hours or overnight. Sprinkle with toasted almonds for garnish and serve with low-fat yoghurt or low-fat sour cream.

NUTRITIONAL VALUES

MINTED RUBY GRAPEFRUIT ICE AND TANGERINE SORBET

SERVES **6**

These two ice cold citrus desserts will definitely get your mouth watering.

MINTED RUBY GRAPEFRUIT ICE

150 g caster sugar

500 ml ruby red grapefruit juice, freshly squeezed, with pulp (4 or 5 grapefruits)

2 tbsp finely chopped mint leaves

mint sprigs to garnish

1 In a small saucepan, heat the sugar with 125 ml of water, stirring until the sugar is dissolved. Boil for 5 minutes. Cool to room temperature, then combine the sugar syrup with the grapefruit juice and the chopped mint leaves.

2 Freeze the mixture in an ice cream maker, following the manufacturer's instructions, or place it in a freezer-proof container and freeze for several hours or overnight. Serve garnished with mint sprigs.

TANGERINE SORBET

100 g caster sugar

2 tbsp finely chopped tangerine or mandarin orange peel, with all white pith removed

500 ml freshly squeezed tangerine juice (about 6–8 tangerines)

1 In a small non-reactive saucepan, combine the sugar, peel, and 125 ml water. Bring the mixture to the boil, stirring until all the sugar has dissolved. Boil for 5 minutes. Remove from heat and allow to cool to room temperature.

2 Combine the syrup with the juice and freeze in an ice cream maker, following the manufacturer's instructions, or place in a freezerproof container and freeze for several hours or overnight before serving.

NUTRITIONAL VALUES

INDEX